MW00586404

THE

JOY

PRACTICE

You are not
responsible for
other peoples.
assumptions
about you —
Be You!
♡ aller

THE

JOY

PRACTICE

*Becoming more of who you are
by experiencing life fully and directly*

ELLEN BROWN ROBINSON

The ALLIANCE for
Indie Publishers

THE JOY PRACTICE: Becoming more of who you are
by experiencing life fully and directly

Ellen Brown Robinson

ISBN-13: 978-0692559017
ISBN-10: 0692559019

The Alliance for Indie Publishers
Indianapolis, Indiana

Copyright © 2015 by Ellen Brown Robinson

The Joy Practice® is a registered trademark.

All rights reserved. No part of this book may be reproduced
without written permission from the publisher, except
by a reviewer who may quote brief passages in a review;
nor may any part of this book be reproduced, stored in a
retrieval system or transmitted in any form or other without
written permission from the publisher.

This book is manufactured in the United States of America.

Editor: Janet Schwind
Designer: Suzanne Parada

For My Soul

For Your Soul

For Her Soul

For His Soul

For the World's Soul

THANK YOU.

Alaric Aloor for helping me feel again.

Katie Wilson Barker for being my first best friend.

Kristen Boice for seeing me. You so see me.

Dorothy Brown–Mom–for your willingness to be uncomfortable so that I can be who I am.

Gene Brown–Dad–for holding the space for me and asking the hard questions.

Brandi Cottingham for handing me a paintbrush and canvas and standing so firmly for me.

Alisa Ervin for being my soft place to land.

Joni Hansen for giving me permission to be who I am when I needed it most.

Kathy McHugh for showing up so vibrantly, mirroring for me my own beauty.

Sally Davis Moore for holding a vision for me that I could not see at the time.

Teresa Morrison for being the best Cranial Sacral Therapist on the planet.

Lindy Richman for that day when you modeled what a boundary was so brilliantly.

Stephen Shields for patiently asking until I got it, 'Have you suffered enough?'

Christie Thrasher-Rudd for bringing the magic of CRT into my life and being an incubator for my heart and soul to take root, expand and bust out.

Maren Robinson for pushing so often and hard on my buttons that I had to finally look at myself.

Miles Robinson for your genuine heart that very quietly and fiercely holds me.

Timothy Robinson for doing all the hard stuff. Soul stuff. You are my Soul Soup Stirrer.

And

Janet Schwind and Suzanne Parada, my edit and design team, for collaborating so beautifully together and with me to bring this beautiful book into being.

From My Joy Bearer

For people, Joy is different. But one Joy that is the same is Love. Love is Joy that some people find at different times in their lives. It may be hard at first but when they find Joy, they will open their heart. It could be hard, it could be easy. But one thing is for sure—all people will experience Joy in their lifetime.

~Maren Robinson

WHAT'S IN HERE

INTRODUCTION

What if there is no end game? What if we can put down our measuring sticks and just breathe? What if we are here to simply experience each moment as fully and directly as we can? And as we do, become more of who we are? And with this, a knowingness that as we become more of who we are, we bless ourselves and the world with our WHOLENESS.

The more I live, the more I recognize this as true. When I can greet life on its terms in each moment, I allow my true nature to surface and I am able to connect to the joy that I am.

•————•

Joy is WHO YOU ARE when you allow yourself
to experience life fully and directly.

•————•

Joy is a state—your natural state! Joy is you being natural...your true nature. What is Joy? For me, Joy is my Soul's anthem. When I engage my Soul, Joy awakens. Joy is the experience you have when you are allowing your authenticity—your true nature—to shine. The Joy Practice then, is just that—a practice that can help you engage with your true nature—your authentic being. The Joy Practice is a way of living. One that brings you into alignment with your true self—your core or essence. So what is Joy? Joy is WHO YOU ARE when you allow yourself to experience life fully and directly.

What do you do when you want to feel better physically? Perhaps you begin to move your body differently or eat differently. By doing something different at a physical level, you will begin to notice the things that have not been working–those foods or types of exercise that are perhaps irritating or inflaming your body. Moving or eating differently can bring your body into its natural state of alignment.

Similarly, it is possible to feel better mentally, emotionally, and spiritually. Just as you can get stuck in a rut with your physical self, it's easy to get stuck in emotional and mental patterns that are not in alignment with the essence of who you are. These patterns can begin to feel limiting and eventually irritate and annoy you. Perhaps even make you mentally and emotionally sick.

The Joy Practice gives a framework that can empower you to come into *resonance* with who you are, which is JOY. It IS within your power to reboot and start anew. A decision to align with your Joy may feel silly, selfish, or perhaps scary. Honor these feelings (and any others!) and the thoughts they bring up in you by FEELING them. And then–do it anyway. Your thoughts and feelings do not have to paralyze you. Your power comes in feeling it all and then jumping. Joy jumps!

Your shift toward JOY begins when you start to notice the thoughts and feelings you are having. Fully conscious, you are empowered to make choices and decisions that resonate and align with your authenticity—your Joy! You can ask yourself, do these thoughts feel good to me? If not, you get to choose new thoughts that feel good to you. Thoughts that feel good to you or resonate with you are thoughts that are aligned with your Joy. As you begin to choose new thoughts that feel good to you, you will naturally begin to let go of thoughts and beliefs that no longer feel good to you. What is happening is that with each choice that feels good, you are consciously becoming more of who you are. You are transforming your mental and emotional patterns and coming into closer alignment with your unique spiritual signature.

So, it's not about finding Joy...it's already there. It's about engaging Joy. As with yoga or any exercise that requires balance, you can achieve that physical balance when you engage the core of your body—the center of you. And so with Joy. Simply imagine a column of white light running through the center of you. That is the core or essence of YOU. And you can engage it at any time and experience your natural state of Joy.

The Essence

My Joy Backstory

———•———

I didn't have to die to have a near-death experience. My experience began with the unplanned statement: "I don't want to live like this anymore." I uttered these words in the summer of 2006. The previous 37 years, I'd been living on autopilot. I did not know this at the time.

The funny thing is, by looking at it, you wouldn't have suspected anything was amiss. It wasn't that my life was bad. By all "standard" measurements, my life was very good. I was married to a wonderful man. I had a great job. I was physically fit and healthy. I was surrounded by loving and caring friends. All good things. Yet these things alone did not make me FEEL alive. I felt dead inside. I would be driving down the street, and I would start crying. There wouldn't have to be anything to jumpstart these tears…they were just so close to the surface. Always. I used to think that this was just who I was. The truth is that I FELT awful. I was miserable. I had all of these things and I FELT so bad. And then, I would feel guilty because I felt bad. Shouldn't someone who has all of these things FEEL good? I was living a life that many people would love to live and I was miserable! My misery was not about the circumstances…my husband, my job, my friends. No. They had nothing to do with it. The misery was caused by my pain. And my pain was caused by holding in my Truth...

What was my Truth? My Truth was and is who I am. I wasn't allowing the beauty that is ME out into the world. I did not feel that my voice mattered. I did not feel that I was a good mother. I did not feel that I was a good daughter. I did not feel that the work I did was sufficient. I could go on. And then something magical happened. I got pregnant with my baby girl, Maren. As I was contemplating how to share this part of my story with you, a dear friend of mine reminded me how I would speak about my pregnancy and the first years of Maren's life. It was a lovely time. So peaceful, sweet, and free. This experience showed me that my life could be different, that I could FEEL differently about my life. And so, I began to make changes so that I would not feel so awful. And ever so slowly, I began to feel better.

"I don't want to live like this anymore." It was speaking this out that woke me up to my life. When I said those life changing words, I was employing the philosophy of Ernest Holmes—and many other spiritual teachers—which is this: By intentionally choosing your thoughts, you can create the reality that is your life. It was an accidental falling into of sorts...I was operating from the seat of my intuitive pants. Almost immediately from my utterance, opportunities—I call them doorways—began to present themselves to help manifest the change I desired. Even though I did not have a name for what I wanted, I desired it so strongly that the energy of it was enough to begin a shift in my life.

My declaration brought me to a girls' night out the following evening, where I found my dear friend Kristen sitting there with a glowing smile on her face. "What's up?" I asked her.

She answered, "I just went to this thing and it's all about possibility."

"I WANT THAT," I declared. About a month later I found myself sitting in a five-day workshop where I got to ask myself this question: What do I want? This was a new experience for me. I had never asked myself this question with intention. It was the beginning of consciously and purposefully designing a life I love. I attended the second five-day workshop and dove deeper. The entire experience culminated with a 90-day workshop during which I got to create three visions for my life.

I remember sitting at my desk in my home office, quieting myself, with just a blank piece of paper in front of me. My intention was to turn off my brain chatter and connect to my intuition. You can do this at any time simply by making the intention to enter your heart space. Your heart space is simply the place inside your chest where you imagine your heart to be. Your heart houses a deep and abiding wisdom that you can always tap into and trust if you desire it.

That day, I asked for my heart to open and to be able to receive the visions. After several moments, three visions came to me. They were, 1) To connect and be free in all of my relationships, 2) To embrace my intuition, and, 3) To inspire others through creative expression.

This was the unleashing of my creativity—of choosing my thoughts with intention. I remember running on a trail by my home and getting this feeling of lightness, like my heart was bursting open. I realized this state of being must be JOY. It was a new and delightful feeling! It was on these runs that I began to unexpectedly "receive" messages. Kind of little downloads of energetic inspirations:

Life is the journey back to ourselves.
Through our vulnerability we find our true strength.
We are cradled in Love.
Our hearts hold the power for transformation.
Let go and live.
Open your heart, change the world.
Choose Love.
Let Love reveal itself.
Love sees clearly.
Love doesn't live in a box.
Love is the portal to peace.
Freedom is living from the heart.
Love is the connection we share with others.
Be gentle with yourself.
The answer lies within.
The answer will come. Listen. Trust.
The Soul speaks. Listen.
Trust and believe that your life is exactly as it is meant to be.
Walk into your imagination and create a masterpiece.

Our greatest responsibility is to be true to ourselves.
Be your Truth.
Authentic is a gift we can be for others.
You are already whole.
Be who you are.
Courageously live your Truth and open the door for others.
When in doubt, lean in.
Relax into the flow of life.
You are beautiful.
Freedom lies in courageous acts inspired by authenticity.

They were like little lightbulbs of Truth. They resonated so with the core of who I was. I wondered, *How
will I get the words out to people?* I knew I needed to share
them with others. It was around this time that my coach
brought paints and canvas to one of our coaching sessions.
Doorway. I said to her, "I don't paint." She simply looked
at me. Moving stubbornly through my resistance, I eventually picked up the paintbrush during that coaching session.
About ten minutes in, I felt that JOY thing. I felt FREE.

Later that summer I was painting with my daughter,
and my sister—the artist—who was also there, said, "She's
doing a faux finish." I had no idea what a faux finish was.
My sister explained that a faux finish is like a layer on top
of a layer. *Doorway.* It was in that moment I realized I could
paint the words that had been so effortlessly coming to
me. Except for that coaching session, I had never painted.
Regardless, I began to create painting after painting. I even
had a technique!

Several months later, my coach called and asked, "When are you going to have your paintings made into cards?" You see, I had that vision of inspiring others through creative expression, coupled with a love of greeting cards and words. "Here are the names of three printers. Call them," she said and hung up. *Doorway.* I called them. The third one with whom I talked offered to take photos of the paintings and then print samples for free. "You're gonna need samples," he said. *Doorway!*

A few weeks later, with my samples in hand, I set out to hit an artsy community in our town to peddle my wares. I can still see me that day and feel the experience... excitement ... nervousness ... anticipation ... I felt so alive! The first place not only put out my samples–my samples–they also asked if I had the original paintings. *Doorway.* My look must have been blank because they said, "You know, to sell?" So, next thing I know, I am selling both the cards and my pieces of inspirational art.

Wow! This was a whole new way of living...identifying what I wanted, which for me was, 1) Being connected and free in my relationships, 2) Embracing my intuition, and, 3) Inspiring others through creative expression. I was doing that!! I wanted more of this juicy goodness. I continued my journey of asking for what I wanted. I can remember claiming various wants...I want to live open hearted, I want to feel better, and I want to live in alignment with my soul.

I distinctly remember one day when I stopped in to visit one of the stores that was selling my cards. I was having a particularly rough day and I said, "I want to find my joy." I see now how these thoughts or intentions were the seeds I planted–the intentional framework for my life. Word by word, sentence by sentence, I have created a life I truly desire and love. It has not been easy and it has not been without an intensity of emotion...feeling ALL of it!

In the fall of 2011 I felt a tug to share with others what I was learning. I was feeling such freedom, personal power, and joy! I was learning that life need not be hard and heavy. And that we (you, me, all!) are meant to experience ease and grace! I wanted others to experience this and share with them how to create their lives intentionally. I felt that I had a lot of what I needed to share the information with others, but I sensed something was missing. Drawn to psychology, I wondered if I was to get my degree in counseling. So I went to check out a local program in my community. It was lovely. And...I was aware that it did not resonate with me. This is an important distinction to note. Just because something is cool doesn't necessarily mean it's your path. Just like some article of clothing might be cool, this doesn't mean you should buy it. All you need to do is check in with your heart. Simply ask, does this resonate with me? Resonation is the feeling you get when you're aligned with your natural state of Joy. Kind of like an "all systems go" awareness.

Later that day, I was in my home and realized the

answer had been right in front of me. A dear friend, Sarah, had gifted me with *The Science of Mind* magazine a couple years earlier. I saw a copy of it sitting on the table and flipped through the pages. In it, I discovered a description of their online classes. *Doorway*. After reading about their offerings, I signed up for their introductory class. It was a fifteen-week online class and, although a bit skeptical—what were these people going to teach me, plus I had never taken an online class—I immediately felt I had come "home."

All that I was learning was in alignment with my life experiences and my intuitive knowing. I felt elated that I was beginning to trust my intuition and that I was receiving the tools I needed to be able to share practically and logically what I sensed, easily with others. Shortly after this, I began to teach workshops in my home called Inspire Your Life! About one year after that, I opened my own creativity studio. I learned many things in the two and a half years I had my studio. One thing I know for sure is that it helped me put into words The Joy Practice, which I am now sharing with the world.

Other People's Joy

—————•

Engaging Joy is the greatest responsibility we have as human beings walking the planet. Why? Because when you are living aligned with your Joy, you are serving with the truest sense of yourself. Yes. That is what I said. When you are authentically YOU, you are serving others. It is the most pure form of altruism, to be your TRUE NATURE. Living in your Joy serves you and, by extension, others. How can it get any better than that? When you go about the business of being YOU, everyone wins. Your Joy is your business. Other people's Joy is their business. Each person gets to choose whether or not they are going to live aligned with their Joy. Said another way, every person on the planet gets to decide if they are going to live in their true nature—their authenticity.

And some people don't choose this. And this is OKAY. And some of those who don't are going to be those you really love and care about. And this is OKAY. And. This can be difficult. It's difficult because once you begin to live according to your true nature—your joy—you will want it for everyone, especially those you love. And. You are not responsible for their Joy. No one else can live or BE some-one else's true nature for them. And. You may be tempted to believe that your Joy depends on another connecting to their Joy. It doesn't. You are a powerhouse. And your power lies in your authenticity. You, experiencing life fully and directly, is you living in your true nature. It is you living your JOY. For a very long time, I felt responsible for the Joy of those around me, especially those closest to me. I didn't even realize it! I became aware that I was actually trying to change myself in order for them to connect with their Joy. Not gonna happen. I learned it was painful to want something for someone more than they wanted it. Even more, it was none of my business! I realized the greatest service I could do for them was to not wish, want, cajole or yearn for them to engage their joy, but for me to engage my Joy. Joy is a choice and we all get to choose.

Origins of Joy, Where it Goes, and How to Get it Back

•————•

Joy alignment is Soul alignment. When you are living aligned with Joy, you are living aligned with your Soul. Joy is not happy bliss all the time. Joy is like an upside-down umbrella that holds all of it–the bliss and the pain. If Joy is your natural state, what happens to it? How do you get disconnected from this natural state of Joy? How do you get out of alignment with your Soul?

It happens almost immediately. From the moment you pop out into this world, you begin the journey away from your natural state of Joy. It's normal and simply part of the human journey. On the journey, you have experiences in which you slowly begin to give parts of yourself away, trading in pieces of your true way of being. Before you know it, you exist far away from your natural state of Joy. I was about fourteen when I lost touch with my Joy. It wasn't that anything specific happened; it was more like the real me went underground. I put on a mask of false joy because it no longer felt safe to be in a world that wanted me to conform. I always felt different–the things I thought about, how I saw the world, the things I was aware of, the feelings I felt, the intensity of the feelings I felt. I didn't feel that who I was would be accepted, so it was safer just to become like everyone else.

In essence, I was disconnecting from my soul, the essence of who I was. In this state of false joy, I was better able to live by the societal paradigms—thoughts, ideas, beliefs, and conditioning—that were my world. By "better able to live by," I mean it was *less painful* in the moment. There was a price, however, because the reality I created was not in alignment with the truth of who I was. It was not in alignment with my Joy, nor my soul. But, it was safe. It became my comfort zone. And it became the reality from which I lived my life. And, it was neither bad nor good. It just was.

Until one day, I tapped into a sense that there was more. The verbal manifestation of this knowing happened in 2006 when I said, "I don't want to live like this anymore." That statement was the thought seed that engaged my soul, the moment I began to awaken my Joy. The years following have been my journey to Joy, to my essence, to me. And, upon reflection, I see that there are steps or practices that have supported me in aligning with my Joy.

Wherever you are in your life right now, know that you can align yourself with your natural state of Joy. And, wherever you are is perfect. Know that everything happens on time! Remember that it has perhaps taken *years* of practicing yourself away from Joy—from who you are—so be gentle with yourself! Whenever you learn something new, especially a new way of being, it takes time and practice. When I began to share The Joy Practice with my clients and they responded so positively, I knew I had to share the ideas more widely. Read the words in this book. Feel them. Keep what resonates and leave the rest. Joy is about becoming more of who you ARE. If these practices help you, great! If you find them restrictive in any way or they do not feel good to you, notice that, too. It's okay. Keep your focus on what YOU want and need—what feels good to you. When something feels good to you, authentically good, this is Soul food. Pay attention!

The Joy Practice In Action

———•———

The practices I share in this book evolved organically in my life and have helped connect me to my natural state of Joy. Looking back, I can see clearly that these practices developed naturally as a result of me choosing from a place of resonance. When something resonates with you, this is a Joy indicator. What does resonance feel like? To me it feels clear, clean, and crisp. Light. When I said, "I don't want to live like this anymore," I was really saying, "I want to live in alignment with my Joy." Or, put another way, I was ready to live in integrity with my Soul.

When you are living aligned with your Joy, you experience ease. It doesn't mean that things are always easy. Easy and ease are two different things. Living with ease is the feeling you get when you can observe your life, allowing it to unfold as it wants to—the good, the bad, the ugly, and the beautiful—no forcing. Not living with ease feels like resistance—kind of like a wall that blocks the natural flow of life. Or like you're dragging a heavy weight chained to your ankle. Life is going to unfold how it wants to because that is the nature of life. Resisting this reality is painful.

Resistance often shows up as fear or a feeling of "stuck-ness." This resistance or stuck-ness is a natural part of the

Joy journey, and so is realizing that there is another choice: Ease! In fact, you are meant to feel good ... to have ease! You can experience ease even when you are in physical or emotional pain. You can do this by allowing the pain to express itself, allowing the flow of life to run through you, with no stuck-ness. I had known this intellectually for the longest time. Meaning, I knew it mentally and in my head, but I hadn't yet converted it into being-ness. It wasn't until a family vacation to the beach that I received the integration of this beautiful gift.

We were meeting up with family. My husband and I annually rent a condo and my husband's sister's family usually stays at a campground. Historically, some of the kids have stayed with us at the condo. Now, I am a person who really likes my space, juxtaposed with an almost neurotic need to take care of others. So...the close quarters of the condo and my *perceived* ideas about what was expected of me had always caused me some anxiety and agitation in previous years. This particular year, my expectation was that two of the kids would be staying with us in the condo. I found out when we got there that four kids in addition to our two were going to be staying in the condo with us. When I realized what was happening, I felt a familiar constriction–a physical, emotional, and intellectual tightening–that constitutes my resistance. Frustration. Anger. Anxiety. The knot had begun to form and tried to lodge itself in my throat. This time, though, instead of ignoring it or repressing it, I allowed the resistance to express itself.

This is key: Instead of my usual, habitual, and patterned behavior, which would have involved whining and complaining to my husband and not letting go of my indignation, I allowed the feelings and thoughts that wanted to be known to express through me–and then let them go.

My thoughts went something like this:

There will be too many people.

They'll eat all the food.

It will be loud.

I won't have enough space for quiet time.

There will be crap all over the place.

ETC., ETC., ETC.

What does this mean, to allow feelings room to express themselves? How is this different from complaining? This is not a spoken expression; it's a deliberate process between you and you. To allow the thought room. First, let the thought come. Don't stuff it back down. Don't try to "just get over it." And then…and this is really important… let the feelings happen. Whether it's anger, heartache, offense, whatever. I allowed all of the feelings that came with the thoughts. It's amazing what happens when you allow feelings–especially those you PERCEIVE as negative ones–the room to express. What I noticed is simply that the feelings did not feel good to me. I was able to look at them in a sort of clinical way, without judgment. By allowing the thoughts, I allowed the feelings. Thoughts and feelings are like little kids; they just want to be noticed and given room to BE!

The third and final step, once you fully allow your thoughts and feelings to express–that is, think your thoughts, feel your feelings–is to then LET THEM GO. Once I did this, it was like a space opened up. I have a name for that space and it's called POSSIBILITY. I did not need to whine and complain to my husband, because I had allowed a space for my thoughts and feelings to air themselves. And in doing so, I now did not feel the need to throw my yucky-feeling emotions out onto others–namely my husband and family. Later the next morning, I was sitting on the beach, toes in sand. I had brought my journal. I asked myself this question: "How did I do that yesterday?" How did I move from an old and familiar pattern of reacting, to a new way of being that involved being still and noticing what was happening within me? My question was answered with the words, "It's a practice." It was like my brain had a screen in it, and these words flashed up on that screen. I immediately recognized that this was so, and that this new way of being had been evolving for some time and was just now making its way into my awareness.

The next question I asked myself was, "What is this practice about?" And what flashed across my brain screen was the word JOY. And then, "It's a Joy Practice." Yes! I realized that this was the Truth. And then I asked, "What does the practice entail?" And, as the answers came to me, I wrote them down in my journal. That journal formed the basis for the next part of this book, which is dedicated to describing The Joy Practice, the nine elements that comprise it, and actual practices or suggestions to help you align with your own natural state of being–your JOY state!

The Joy Practice Paradigm

———•———

So how do you come into union or alignment with your Joy? Practice, baby! Joy is a practice. This may seem odd–a practice to become who you are. I had a dear friend say to me very vehemently, "It's not a practice!" I understood where she was coming from; I understood that the idea of a "practice" did not resonate with her. And, that was and is okay. This is my Truth, my Joy. None of it, some of it, or all of it may resonate with you. TRUST what doesn't and TRUST what does. My experience is that this coming back into alignment with my true self or my essence, has been and is a practice–a discipline. Just like when you start a new exercise regimen. It is and also has been a process. A process of getting to know ME. My Joy or my Meness, when I distill it, can be described by the following nine words. I call them "Elements": Creativity, Aliveness, Possibility, Gratitude, Compassion, Abundance, Peace, Freedom, and Vulnerability. And, the process of truly embracing these elements included a *moving away* from one reality or paradigm that included *these* beliefs, which were no longer true:

1) I am powerless to change my life.

2) Feelings are scary and I avoid them.

3) It's best to be in control; when I'm in control I know what to expect.

4) Life happens TO me; I am the victim of circumstance.

5) When I take care of my needs, I am being selfish.

6) I am not enough.

7) Life is stressful and anxiety ridden–I just have to deal with it.

8) Things must be a certain way in order for me to feel good about me/life.

9) I am NOT safe.

...To another reality or paradigm that includes *these* truths:

1) I can create a life I love through intentional thought!

2) Feelings CAN be scary AND they are amazing and I feel them and celebrate them!

3) Anything is possible when I'm open!

4) My life happens FOR me; everything is a gift!

5) Loving myself, I become WHOLE!

6) I am more than enough; I am a gift!

7) I can cultivate internal peace.

8) Freedom lies in my ability to let go of what or how I thought "it" would be!

9) I am Held.

Each of these nine truths makes manifest–*brings into being*–one of the nine elements of Joy. Did any of the above nine truth statements resonate with you? Make you uncomfortable? Which ones? It is with these truths that you can begin to practice connecting with Joy. Whichever truth resonated with you MOST or scared you MOST, that's where I encourage you to start. It takes a decision to have a new experience. It also takes an immense amount of courage to move out of a paradigm, way of thinking, that's comfortable and even perhaps feels safe, but has outgrown its usefulness. You may not yet actually believe with your mind statements one through nine that comprise The Joy Practice. Yet your heart and Soul will feel and know if the beliefs resonate deep within you.

As you'll read about in the next section, each of the above nine truths connects to one of the nine elements. Each element has a practical activity, an actual step to help you move toward your Joy–tools you can put to use right now. Because Joy isn't all in your head. Joy is real and you can bring it into being in your life. Use these practices in the way that works for you. Use all nine. Use one. Use several. The practices are designed to let you engage in one practice per week. You can also switch this up...do one practice for three weeks or a month or six weeks. And then move on. Start with the first one or start with the fifth one. The Joy Practice is here to help you so do what feels GOOD to YOU.

Let's. Do. This.

The Practice

Element:	**CREATIVITY**
Core Belief:	**I can create a life I love through intentional thought.**
Practice:	**Claim it!**

Creativity is always a leap of faith. You're faced with a blank page, blank easel, or an empty stage.

~Julia Cameron

———•———

The Big Bang is not a has-been. The Big Bang is available at any moment, at any time. In each moment, we have the opportunity to CREATE, to INNOVATE, to BRING INTO BEING that which has never been before. The Big Bang IS Creativity. And, it is not something that is reserved for a precious few as I used to believe. Yes, creativity is artistic and expressive such as painting, writing, and acting. AND it is so much more! Our life is our canvas, our stage, our blank page! By creativity I mean that we—*you, me, all*—are literally MADE OF life force energy... the energy that makes up the cosmos. You are source energy. As source energy, you have the power to create anything you desire. All you need ask yourself is this: What will I create today? You create in each moment through the thoughts you choose to think.

If you need a visual, think of a flower bulb being planted in the earth. Each one of your beliefs or thoughts is like a flower bulb—a SEED that you plant. A flower bulb is nurtured by the sun and the rain, nature's emotions. Eventually, the flower bulb begins to create roots, grow, and eventually shoot out of the ground, fully manifested in physical form as a flower, perhaps a tulip. And so with your thoughts. As you choose your thoughts, you are planting them in energetic soil. You do this whether you are conscious OR unconscious of the thoughts you choose. Then, just as the sun and the rain cultivate and grow that flower bulb, your emotions—how you feel about your thought—literally wrap that thought energetically and build an emotional framework around it that help that thought grow. The emotional framework evolves that thought into BEING. For example, when I created the thought and vision—I inspire people through creative expression—I felt giddy, excited, bliss!! The thought of doing that was so joyful and wonderful to me! What is it that you WANT to bring into being in your life? All you need to do is consciously select the thought and then FEEL what it will be like when that IDEA comes into fruition for you!

Isn't it empowering?! By being present and conscious, you get to CREATE a life you love by choosing thoughts that feel good to you. Suffering and misery come when you continue to think thoughts that have outlived their purpose in your life. Remember how I used to live? I was the one making myself miserable by continuing to think thoughts that did not feel good. I became aware that they had become habitual patterns of thought that felt bad to me. It is possible to FEEL BETTER. You can dare to create a new experience today. You can dare to think a new thought–one that feels good to you! Trust the thoughts that come to you that feel good, and know they will manifest in a way that aligns with your JOY. When you begin to shed old ways of thinking, you are making room for the newness that wants to be expressed in your life. You have the opportunity to create anew in each moment. Let's practice!

PRACTICING CREATIVITY – Claim it!

What You'll Need:

- ☑ Quiet space @ the beginning of the day
- ☑ 15 minutes
- ☑ 3x5 index cards
- ☑ Journal/paper and pen
- ☑ Be-YOU-tiful YOU

Please note that the practice is NOT about the journaling. The practice is to Claim It! The journaling is simply a tool to help support the core practice. The practice is about claiming what you want. When you first begin to practice, it might seem awkward. You may not know what you want, or even how to determine what it is you want. So, I've provided some questions in bold for each of the seven days to help get you started. You may wish to abandon my questions mid-week and begin claiming your own wants. This is perfectly okay. Claiming what you want is the practice for Creativity. Finally, at the end of each day, I ask you to reflect on your day and how, if at all, what you claimed manifested for you. In some instances, the questions will be the same or similar. Try not to get caught up in the questions at the end of the day. The key is the reflective time so that you can begin to see a connection between claiming what it is you want and what actually manifests in your life.

Day 1 Creativity

When you get up this morning, find a quiet spot. Imagine that in your mind there is a switch. Turn OFF that switch. Imagine that in your heart there is a switch. Turn ON that switch. Breathe in and out, slowly, for a few minutes. Allow your thoughts to come spontaneously in response to the question: **What will I create today?** Imagine your heart opening to receive the answers; you can trust these messages as they come from the soul through the heart. The messages may come in the form of words, feelings, impressions, colors...there are no limitations. Write down in your journal the information you receive. This is the most important part—you are CLAIMING what it is you want. After this process, say thank you, put the journal away, and go about your day. You may wish to write that which you are claiming for the day on an index card that you can carry with you during your day to remind you of your practice. For example: *Today, I am creating peace in all* *of my interactions with people.* When your day is finished, take a few moments to reflect...did your day manifest what you imagined you were going to create? If yes, how? Other insights? Write down any thoughts that come to you in your journal.

Day 2 Creativity

When you get up this morning, find a quiet spot. Imagine that in your mind there is a switch. Turn OFF that switch. Imagine that in your heart there is a switch. Turn ON that switch. Breathe in and out, slowly, for a few minutes. Allow your thoughts to come spontaneously in response to the question: **What kind of day will I create today?** Imagine your heart opening to receive the answers; you can trust these messages. The messages may come in the form of words, feelings, impressions, colors...there are no limitations. Write down in your journal the information you receive. This is the most important part–you are CLAIMING what it is you want. After this process, say thank you, put the journal away, and go about your day. You may wish to write down the kind of day you are claiming today on an index card that you can carry with you during your day to remind you of your practice. For example: *Today, I am claiming a day that is filled with laughter and ease.* When your day is finished, take a few moments to reflect how, if at all, your day reflected what you imagined you were going to create. If it did, how? How did you feel throughout the day? How do you feel now? Write down in your journal anything that resonated with you or that sticks out for you.

Day 3 Creativity

When you get up this morning, find a quiet spot. Imagine that in your mind there is a switch. Turn OFF that switch. Imagine that in your heart there is a switch. Turn ON that switch. Breathe in and out, slowly, for a few minutes. Allow your thoughts to come spontaneously in response to the question: **How do I want to experience today?** This is the most important part–you are CLAIM-ING what it is you want. Imagine your heart opening to receive the answers; you can trust these messages. The messages may come in the form of words, feelings, impres-sions, colors…there are no limitations. Write down in your journal the information you receive. After this process, say thank you, put the journal away, and go about your day. You may wish to write down the kind of experience you are claiming today on an index card that you can carry with you during your day to remind you of your practice. For example: *Today, I want to experience my business meeting as focused and effective.* When your day is finished, take a few moments to reflect…did what you say you wanted to expe-rience manifest? How? What was it like? Did you notice your feelings? What thoughts did you have?

Day 4 Creativity

When you get up this morning, find a quiet spot.

Imagine that in your mind there is a switch. Turn OFF that switch. Imagine that in your heart there is a switch. Turn ON that switch. Breathe in and out, slowly, for a few minutes. Allow your thoughts to come spontaneously in response to the question: **How do I want to BE today?** This is the most important part–you are CLAIMING what it is you want. Imagine your heart opening to receive the answers; you can trust these messages. The messages may come in the form of words, feelings, impressions, colors… there are no limitations. Write down in your journal the information you receive. After this process, say thank you, put the journal away, and go about your day. You may wish to write down how it is that you want to BE today on an index card that you can carry with you during your day to remind you of your practice. For example: *Today, I want to be deliberate and intentional in all of my interactions.* When your day is finished, take a few moments to reflect…was how you wanted to BE today brought to life in your day? Be aware of any of the ways this might have come to fruition. It might not look like what you thought it was going to look like. Be open to the possibilities. Write down any thoughts or feelings that are or were especially unique or different for you in your journal.

Day 5 Creativity

When you get up this morning, find a quiet spot. Imagine that in your mind there is a switch. Turn OFF that switch. Imagine that in your heart there is a switch.

Turn ON that switch. Breathe in and out, slowly, for a few minutes. Allow your thoughts to come spontaneously in response to the question: **How do I want others to experience me today?** This is the most important part—you are CLAIMING what it is you want. Imagine your heart opening to receive the answers; you can trust these messages. The messages may come in the form of words, feelings, impressions, colors...there are no limitations. Write down in your journal the information you receive. After this process, say thank you, put the journal away, and go about your day. You may wish to write down the way you want others to experience you today on an index card that you can carry with you during your day to remind you of your practice. For example: *Today, I would like others to experience me as calm and reassuring.* When your day is finished, take a few moments to reflect...did you receive any feedback from others that would affirm that what you wanted came into being today? If yes, what was the feedback? How did it feel? If not, in what other ways do you or might you know that how you wanted others to receive you, in fact, was the case? Write down in your journal any thoughts or feelings that come to you in response to these questions.

Day 6 Creativity

When you get up this morning, find a quiet spot. Imagine that in your mind there is a switch. Turn OFF that switch. Imagine that in your heart there is a switch. Turn ON that switch. Breathe in and out, slowly, for a few minutes. Allow your thoughts to come spontaneously in response to the question: **How do I want to experience ME today?** This is the most important part–you are CLAIMING what it is you want. Imagine your heart opening to receive the answers; you can trust these messages. The messages may come in the form of words, feelings, impressions, colors...there are no limitations. Write down in your journal the information you receive. After this process, say thank you, put the journal away, and go about your day. You may wish to write down how you would like to experience yourself today on an index card that you can carry with you during your day to remind you of your practice. For example: *Today, I would like to experience myself as confident.* When your day is finished, take a few moments to reflect...did how you want to experience yourself come into being during your day? If so, how did it feel to experience yourself in the way you wanted? If not, how did you experience yourself? How did this feel? Write down in your journal any thoughts or feelings that come in response to these questions.

Day 7 Creativity

When you get up this morning, find a quiet spot. Imagine that in your mind there is a switch. Turn OFF that switch. Imagine that in your heart there is a switch. Turn ON that switch. Breathe in and out, slowly, for a few minutes. Allow your thoughts to come spontaneously in response to the question: **What is my heart's deepest desire?** This is the most important part–you are CLAIMING what it is you want. Imagine your heart opening to receive the answers; you can trust these messages. The messages may come in the form of words, feelings, impressions or colors. Write down in your journal the information you receive. After this process, say thank you, put the journal away, and go about your day. Write down the answers you get to the question, *What is my heart's deepest desire?* on an index card. This time, tape the card to your bathroom mirror or put it somewhere that you are sure to see it often. For example: *My deepest heart's desire is to have deeply connected relationships and a job I enjoy so much I jump out of bed to go there every day.* This practice will continue for as long as you want it to… whenever you see that index card on your mirror or wherever you decide to put it, say the words that are your deepest heart's desire. Allow yourself to feel what it will feel like when your heart's deepest desire comes into being. Repeat. Depending on what your heart's deepest desire is, it could manifest in a day or it might take a year. What you can be sure of is that when you CLAIM what it is you want, you are planting a seed. Your feelings provide the emotional framework to make that seed grow. And, your thought seed WILL manifest. The rest of The Joy Practice elements will help you navigate as you progress along your journey in Creativity.

Element: **ALIVENESS**

Core Belief: **Feelings CAN be scary AND they are amazing and I feel them and celebrate them!**

Practice: **Feel it!**

Nothing is as important as my aliveness.

~Shiela Dimof

● ———— ●

What is ALIVENESS? Just because you are breathing does not mean you are alive. Aliveness is the courage to feel life as it happens. This takes courage because sometimes life happening brings with it feelings of sadness, anger, frustration, and pain. These are feelings that you have possibly been trained to see as "bad." I remember growing up, one of the messages I received was, "Don't get too excited." This could be about anything... going on vacation, Halloween, making a sports team. The underlying message I received was that it was important to avoid feeling disappointment at all costs.

As I've evolved, I have had to teach myself and allow myself to FEEL excitement...to BE excited about something. It has become WORTH it to me to FEEL the excitement. If I get excited about something and then get a result that I had not anticipated, I allow myself to be disappointed. I now know that this is okay. If you can and if it feels true for you, try viewing the feelings that many people (perhaps you) have been conditioned to see as "bad" as simply one end of what I call the Aliveness spectrum. The extent to which you're willing to feel this end of the Aliveness spectrum directly correlates to how intensely you will feel the opposite end of the spectrum: feelings like bliss, happiness, ease, grace, freedom, peace. Both ends offer a sense of Aliveness! Commit to living Alive! You are worth it! Lean into your fear of feeling. Acknowledge, that, hell yes, this is scary!! And do it anyway.

It is possible to feel your way to Aliveness. Yes! You will feel disappointment. Yes! You will feel anxiety. Yes! You will feel bitterness. And....you will also feel connection! Harmony! And grace! Every feeling is VALID. You can learn to relish and revel in ALL of the glorious feelings that are available to you, and your soul will sing! You are meant to feel *good*, yes! And, learning to feel ALL of your feelings is a launch pad for feeling the way you want. You cannot hedge your bets when you make the choice to live in alignment with JOY. You cannot simultaneously guard yourself from disappointment AND live in Aliveness. Let's practice!

PRACTICING ALIVENESS

What You'll Need:

- ☑ Quiet space @ the beginning of the day
- ☑ 15 minutes
- ☑ 3x5 index cards
- ☑ Journal/paper and pen
- ☑ Be-YOU-tiful YOU

Day 1 Aliveness

I once had a client who painted a painting and on it she wrote: "Nothing is as important as my aliveness." Wow. I've used this affirmation myself when I seem to lose my way, unable to feel my own compass, and feeling a bit numb. So, today, after you get up, find your bathroom mirror. Say into the mirror, looking at yourself, **Nothing is as important as my aliveness.** Say it again, more strongly. Say it one more time, as convicted as possible. Throughout the day, simply repeat, **NOTHING IS AS IMPORTANT AS MY ALIVENESS.** See what unfolds. You may find it helpful to write down this affirmation on an index card or somewhere that you will see it throughout your day to remind you. At the end of your day, take about 10 minutes for some reflection. Was this practice easy or difficult for you? How did it feel for you to focus on Aliveness today? How do you feel right now? Did you notice a difference to your day? If so, what was it? Can you describe it? Write down in your journal any thoughts or feelings you get in response to these questions.

Day 2 Aliveness

Set aside 15-20 minutes to do this practice this morning. Find a quiet spot. Sit quietly with your eyes closed. Take a few moments to allow the thoughts and feelings you might be having. When I say "allow," what I mean is, let yourself have them. Be aware if you are denying or repressing a feeling or thought. Be as aware as you can be. Allow yourself to notice the thoughts and feelings, and then let them go. No need to hang on. Now, pull up a memory or a time that you were giddy with anticipation of what was to come. If you have trouble, know that you can always ask for help in remembering. Literally, say, "Please help me remember a time that I was giddy with anticipation of something that was to come." And then, wait for the answer to come. Perhaps it was when you were a child, or maybe a time more recently. If a memory or thought does not present itself, perhaps an event has happened in your life that delighted you and brought you much joy. Tap into the feelings of this event. Let these feelings expand within you and as you do, feel the details of the event itself dissolve and let the feelings take over—perhaps it is giddiness, anticipation, delight, and joy. Follow the feelings as they expand from your heart and begin to permeate your different body parts...the lungs, the stomach, the torso, the arms, the fingers, the hips, the legs, the feet, the brain, and eventually all of the cells in your body. Feel the Aliveness in each body part. Eventually, feel your entire body pulsating as the feelings buzz and dance in you–alive! Let yourself feel this Aliveness for at least 5 minutes. When the time is up, finish your Aliveness Meditation by saying thank you to your body, and then go about your day. At the end of the day, take about 5 or 10 minutes for reflection. How did you feel about the Aliveness meditation? Did it have an impact on your day? If so, what was it? How do you feel now? Write down in your journal any thoughts or feelings that you receive in response to these questions.

Day 3 Aliveness

After you get up, find your bathroom mirror. Say into the mirror, looking at yourself, **I am alive. Here and now. I am alive. How can I live MORE alive?** Throughout the day, simply repeat, **I AM ALIVE. HOW CAN I LIVE MORE ALIVE?** See what unfolds. You may find it helpful to write down this question on an index card or somewhere that you will see it throughout your day to remind you. You don't need to KNOW how to live more alive. Being in the *question* of how you can live more alive is enough. The question will invite the answers. Your job is to be open to the answers as they present themselves during your day. At the end of your day take about 10 minutes to reflect. How did you feel today? Did you feel alive? Did you feel numb? Did you feel a mix of both? What was your experience like for you? What are you feeling now?

Write down in your journal any thoughts or feelings you receive in response to these questions.

Day 4 Aliveness

Read through this entire practice before you begin. When you get up this morning, find a quiet and comfortable spot. Lay down on a couch, bed, or yoga mat or wherever is most comfortable. Make sure you are by yourself. Today's practice is called "Thank you, body." Beginning with your feet, bring into your awareness a feeling of Aliveness within the cells of your feet. By that I mean, feel your cells in your feet dancing and buzzing. Feel them pulsate—they are so alive! You can also visualize this awareness by *seeing* the cells in your feet with little tiny faces on them. After a couple of minutes of this awareness of your feet, say aloud or to yourself, "Thank you, feet." Moving up your body, stopping at the parts you are moved to stop at, continue feeling the aliveness within each body part and seeing the cells with smiling faces, saying "thank you" to that body part. Remember to thank the internal body parts too, such as the heart, lungs, stomach, and kidneys. If it feels good to you, you may choose to add a reason why you are thankful, something like, "Thank you, heart, for pumping blood through my body and helping me to feel." The two most important things about this practice are, 1) Make it your own. Follow your gut. You cannot do this wrong. And, 2) Allow whatever feelings that want to be expressed the room to be expressed, meaning, try not to suppress or deny the feelings as they come up. All feelings are valid and are part of your Aliveness. This can be a very feeling practice with much emotion. Allow it. Be with it. You are safe.

When you are finished, drink some water and then go about your day. At the end of your day spend a few minutes reflecting. How did the Thank You, Body exercise impact you and your experience today? Do you feel any kind of connection with your body that you did not feel before? How did you feel during the exercise, during the day, and now? Write down in your journal any thoughts or feelings you receive in response to these questions.

Day 5 Aliveness

After you get up, find your bathroom mirror. Looking into the mirror at yourself, say, **I am willing to feel all of life. The highs and the lows. The ups and the downs. I find my Aliveness in feeling it all.** Repeat this affirmation several times and with conviction. Then, throughout the day, say to yourself, **I AM WILLING TO FEEL IT ALL.** You may find it helpful to write down this affirmation on an index card or somewhere that you will see it throughout your day to remind you. At the end of your day take about 10 minutes to reflect. How did your day go today? Were you able to let yourself feel? Was it uncomfortable? Comfortable? How do you feel now? Write down in your journal any thoughts and feelings you receive in response to these questions.

Day 6 Aliveness

Today is about noticing. Notice your willingness to feel or not to feel. When you are feeling a so-called "negative" feeling, stop yourself. Take a deep breath. Then, what you are going to do next is imagine the feeling moving through your heart. Literally, see or visualize the feeling on the bottom of your heart and then be with it as it moves through your heart. Then, see or visualize the feeling as it comes out at the top of your heart. So, if the feeling is annoyance, see annoyance hanging out at the bottom of your heart. Give annoyance a symbol or see it as the small letter "a." See annoyance as it makes its way through your amazing, beautiful, and healing heart. Once it pops out the other side, say thank you.

What you are doing is transmuting a "negative" feeling into LOVE using your heart. That is what the heart does—it transmutes FEAR—all perceived negativity—into LOVE. Once you do this, a space of possibility opens up in the space that was once occupied by that "negative" feeling. It is the space of Love. At the end of your day, take about 10 minutes to reflect. Were you able to notice when you were having a "negative" feeling? Were you able to consciously stop yourself and do the practice of working the feeling through your heart? How did it feel? Did you have any "a-ha's"? How do you feel right now? Write down in your journal any thoughts or feelings you receive in response to these questions.

Day 7 Aliveness

Today, you are recommitting to your Aliveness. Today, after you get up, go to your bathroom mirror. Say into the mirror, looking at yourself, **Nothing is as important as my aliveness.** Throughout the day, simply repeat, **NOTHING IS AS IMPORTANT AS MY ALIVE-NESS.** It might be helpful for you to write the affirmation on a 3x5 index card to remind you of your practice today. See what unfolds. At the end of your day, take about 10 minutes to reflect. After a week of practicing Aliveness, do you notice anything different about yourself? What does Aliveness mean to you? How might you carry the practice of Aliveness with you into the next weeks and months? Write down in your journal any thoughts and feelings you receive in response to these questions.

Element:	**POSSIBILITY**
Core Belief:	**Anything is possible when I'm open**
Practice:	**Allow it!**

*A thought, even a possibility,
can shatter and transform us.*

~Friedrich Nietzsche

• ———— •

The third element of The Joy Practice is Possibility. And the practice is called Allow. What do I mean by "allow"? Allowing says YES to life. Allowing is *letting life in*! Is your first response to a new person or opportunity or idea a "yes" or a "no"? When you say "no" and "but," you are putting up an energetic wall between you and what wants to be. When someone or something comes into your life, it's because there is a possibility that lives there. Living in possibility is about being OPEN–living life with an open heart and open mind. A great affirmation to manifest living in possibility is: I AM OPEN.

I remember when I first started to open up to possibility, the thing I noticed the most was new feelings and thoughts that wanted room to express themselves in me. It took a lot of courage to feel these new feelings and think these new thoughts. It is an extremely important component of Joy because it is the beginning of how we let go of a way of thinking that is no longer working for us. When I started to let new thoughts and feelings in, it was so powerful because it provided a space or an opening for magic to happen…the place of Possibility.

It was some time after I had claimed, *I don't want to live like this anymore* when my husband and I began to have a very difficult time. It wasn't WHAT was happening that was making things difficult; it was how I FELT about what was happening.

So, I began to notice the thoughts that were causing me stress and anxiety. I noticed one of those thoughts was that I HAD to stay married. Being raised Catholic, this was the belief that was instilled in me. This belief was one of the values that was contained in the paradigm—*way of thinking*—that I grew up with. And…it was causing me stress and anxiety! So, I did what Possibility invites and I chose to think a new thought. One that more closely aligned to ME and my Joy. I chose the thought: I don't HAVE to stay married. Well, woo wee! All of a sudden I was not stressed or anxious. It appeared that this new thought was more ME. By choosing a thought that felt better—that was MORE authentic to who I was—the space of Possibility presented itself. I felt like I could breathe! This thought did not mean we were not going to stay married. And I did not choose it as a license for divorce or to not stay married. No.

I chose it because it felt better to me. What it did was give me SPACE. I was loving ME by giving ME room to see things differently–to gain a different perspective. Choosing this thought was me choosing Joy. Joy is a choice.

So, what keeps possibility out? Fear, that's what. Fear of the unknown, of doing something differently, or of knowing someone or something differently. I know my husband differently and more intimately than ever before because I was willing to think a new thought, one that was really scary for me. It was such a gift because the thought opened up conversation and a place of vulnerability I had not visited in myself or in our relationship.

Fear keeps you bound to the known. And this is okay. Until it's not anymore. Know that fear is your friend. Why? Because when you feel it, it is an indication that there is something more for you there, beneath the surface. Fear is normal and natural and helpful when you use it as the TOOL that it was intended to be. Fear is there to move you FORWARD. Everyone has fear. And, feeling your fear is important to living in Possibility.

Fear is there to move you FORWARD.

Often, fear is covering up some other feelings that you might be avoiding…pain, grief, disappointment, sadness, anger, resentment, or frustration. When you allow yourself to feel the fear, this very act opens up a space for whatever is there to come to the surface. Feeling your fear will bring you to Possibility. Possibility is living life as an adventure… in wonderment, awe, and curiosity about what's next. Whenever your desire for adventure and curiosity over-takes your fear of the unknown, you are more willing to say yes and live in Possibility. Without hesitation, Yes! I am not saying no is never warranted or that you should not draw personal boundaries. That is another topic. What I am referring to here is that the more you say yes to life, the more aligned you are with the core of WHO YOU ARE… the more aligned you are with YOU—with your JOY. Let's practice!

PRACTICING POSSIBILITY

What You'll Need:

- ☑ Quiet space @ the end of the day
- ☑ 15 minutes
- ☑ 3x5 index cards
- ☑ Journal/paper and pen
- ☑ Be-YOU-tiful YOU

Day 1 Possibility

As you begin your day, look at yourself in the mirror and set an intention for possibility. Today's claim is: **My heart is open to the possibilities of this day.** Say it several more times with conviction and confidence. Throughout the day, repeat, **I AM OPEN**. It may be helpful to write the affirmation, *I am open,* on a 3x5 index card to carry with you through the day to remind you of your practice. See what unfolds. At the end of your day, spend about 10 minutes reflecting on your day. Did you notice anything different or out of the ordinary today? Did any thought or idea particularly intrigue you? What surprised or delighted you? What frustrated or annoyed you? How did you feel? How do you feel right now? Write down in your journal any thoughts or feelings you receive in response to these questions.

Day 2 Possibility

Today's practice is to notice when you say no. This could be a verbal "no" or an energetic no. An energetic no is when you don't use any words but you can feel your whole body kind of scrunch up and you feel yourself closing off to something or someone. Just notice. You may want to write down the words, *Notice when I verbally or nonverbally say no today,* on a 3x5 index card to carry with you throughout the day to remind you of your practice. At the end of your day, spend about 10 minutes in reflection. Were you able to notice when you gave a verbal or nonverbal no? If yes, how did it feel? What were the situations when you felt yourself *say* no? Did you feel expansive or constricted? What thoughts did you have about yourself or the situation when you experienced yourself saying no? How do you feel now? Write down in your journal any thoughts or feelings you receive in response to these questions.

Day 3 Possibility

As you begin your day, look at yourself in the mirror and say: **I am open to what this day brings; I am excited for the miracles that are sure to unfold.** Repeat this statement several times, with conviction and passion. And then, say to yourself throughout the day: **I EXPERIENCE MIRACLES HAPPENING ALL AROUND ME.** It may be helpful to write this affirmation, *I experience miracles happening all around me,* on a 3x5 index card to carry with you throughout your day to remind you of your practice. At the end of your day, take about 10 minutes to reflect upon your day. Did you experience anything new? Did you have any insights—an insight is a thought you've never had before or a way of thinking about something or someone that gives you a new perspective that is inspiring to you. How did you feel throughout the day? How do feel right now? Write down in your journal any thoughts or feelings you receive in response to these questions.

Day 4 Possibility

Today is about being open to new experiences. Try something completely new to you today. For example, order something different for lunch, drive a new route, smile and say hello to someone you don't know, hold someone's hand, ask for help, call someone instead of texting them. It may be helpful to write down on a 3x5 index card the following, *Do something completely new today,* to carry with you throughout your day and remind you about your practice. At the end of your day, take about 10 minutes to reflect upon your day. What did you do differently? How did it feel? What emotions did you experience? How are you feeling now? Write down in your journal any thoughts or feelings you receive in response to these questions.

Day 5 Possibility

As you begin your day, look at yourself in the mirror and ask yourself these questions: **What would my day be like if I truly believed that anything is possible? What would I do *today* if I truly believed anything is possible?** It may be helpful to write down the question, *What would I do today if I truly believed anything is possible?* on a 3x5 index card to carry with you throughout your day to remind you of your practice. At the end of your day, take about 10 minutes to reflect on your day. Did the thought cross your mind during the day? Did you do anything different today? How did you feel throughout the day? How do you feel right now? Write down in your journal any thoughts or feelings you receive in response to these questions.

Day 6 Possibility

Today is about noticing. It's a little bit like when you buy a certain kind of car, then you start noticing everyone on the road who owns the same car. You may have never seen them before but now all of a sudden you notice they are everywhere. Likewise, today, with an open heart and mind, notice any synchronicities, any seeming coincidences in your day. Keep your mind intentioned to see these situations. Look for things that "click." It may be helpful for you to write the reminder, *Today is about noticing synchronicities*, on a 3x5 index card to carry with you throughout the day to remind you of your practice. At the end of your day, take 10 minutes to reflect on your day. What stood out to you? Write down in your journal any thoughts or feelings you receive in response to this question.

Day 7 Possibility

You are always held. Just the other day at Target, I lost my phone. I repeated to myself, "I am held. I know this will work out." It did. I went to customer service and someone had turned in my phone. These happenings are not chance. They happen because of the beliefs you choose to believe in your life and on any given day. So, today is about becoming consciously aware of being held. You may be asking yourself, *Held by what exactly?* That is a good question. It is for you to insert the word that feels right to you...for me it is a mixture—Love, God, energy, the Universe, my Soul—you get the picture. I actually visualize or see a big web of support, holding me as I go throughout my day. So, as you begin your day, look at yourself in the mirror and say, **Anything is possible. I go about**

my day knowing I am supported always, in all ways. Throughout your day, say to yourself, **ANYTHING IS POSSIBLE. I AM SUPPORTED**. It may be helpful for you to write down the statement, *Anything is possible. I am supported,* on a 3x5 index card to carry with you throughout the day to remind you of your practice. At the end of the day, take 10 minutes to reflect on your day. Were you able to let yourself feel held? How did that feel? Did anything special happen that made you aware of this notion of being held? How did it feel? How do you feel now? Write down any thoughts or feelings you receive in response to these questions.

Element: **GRATITUDE**

Core Belief: **My life happens FOR me;
              everything is a gift.**

Practice: **Say thank you! No matter what.**

*If the only prayer you said was thank you,
that would be enough.*

~Meister Eckhart

•————•

What is gratitude? It is a way of being that welcomes everything. The good. The bad. The ugly. The beautiful. How do you get to gratitude? SAY THANK YOU NO MATTER WHAT. That is the practice for Gratitude. I understand. Sometimes you just don't feel grateful. Neither do I. That's why I say thank you. No matter what. It ALWAYS gets me to be grateful in an authentic way. The more you can appreciate and be grateful for ALL of the things, people, and events in your life, the more you will see that everything does happen FOR you. It is a gift. It is ALL a gift.

Saying thank you no matter what is a magic-maker. That's what I said. Saying thank you no matter what catapults you into the realm of magic and miracles. Want miracles? Say thank you. No matter what. The thunderstorm I am caught in? Thank you. My car wreck? Thank you. My divorce? Thank you. My spouse cheating on me? Thank you. The happiness, the sadness, the anger, the bliss, the frustration, my child who is being unruly, my cancer diagnosis. All of it. Thank you. You don't have to LIKE the shitty stuff because life sure is shitty sometimes. And, it's perfectly okay to say, "Fuck this!" And, in the next breath you can say, "Thank you!"

Not too long ago, I became conscious of some fear I was carrying around with me. And it made me REALLY mad. I was pissed OFF! And, you know what I did? I shouted, "Fuck this!" And that still wasn't enough, so I went and painted the words. I felt so much better. And then you know what I did? I said thank you for the word fuck. Thank you ALWAYS elevates you. It doesn't matter WHAT you are saying thank you for–just that you are saying it.

Why is gratitude so magical? Saying thank you raises your vibration. Each of us lives at a certain energetic vibration. When that vibration rises, you feel better. As your vibration rises, you will begin to notice more and more miracles or synchronicities happening in your life. Saying thank you brings more of what you want into your life. About a year ago, I set my iPhone facedown beside my bed. My nightly glass of water was next to it. I had the fleeting thought that I'd better move my phone, but I did not heed the thought. In the morning, water had condensed on my glass and had puddled on the floor. I picked up my iPhone and saw that the water had gotten inside of it. I took the phone to a guy to be fixed. This guy was rumored to be able to fix anything iPhone-related. He took one look at my phone and said, "Yeah, I can't fix that."

I left the place. I began to panic. I did not have the funds to purchase a new iPhone at the time. This wasn't just any phone, it was my *everything* phone–work, personal, kids... I started to worry that I wouldn't be able to connect with anyone and that I'd miss important information. Are you noticing the thoughts I was choosing to think? As I worked the practice for Possibility, which is to allow, I began to feel my panic and anxiety–important. Why was this important? Because I allowed room for the FEELINGS to rise up in me and I FELT them. This allowed Possibility to show up. I took a deep breath. And remembered. All I need to do is say thank you. I reminded myself that everything that happens in my life is for me, a gift. That everything that happens is about expansion...that's expanding, getting bigger! And I began to relax. I did not know why this had happened, but I was choosing to see it as a gift. And P.S. I still have this iPhone. It *magically* fixed itself.

When you have a situation like this or something even more potentially life-altering, like a divorce or losing joy, when you can say, "Thank you. I don't know how, but I know this experience is for me. I know it is about expansion in my life," you will feel better and your energetic vibration–how you BE in the world–will elevate. Again, it is not about slapping on a mask of falseness. Joy is not about being fake. It is about being true—true to you. Feeling ALL of your feelings, fully and directly. Feel it all... the anger, the sadness, the frustration, the judgment, the bitterness, the panic, the anxiety, AND the joy, the bliss, the love, the compassion, the excitement AND be thankful for it ALL. You are the one who gets to decide whether or not you choose to see your life, all of it, as a gift. You can do so simply by claiming it (see Creativity, Practice #1) with something like: **I choose to believe my life and everything in it happens FOR me and is a gift!** Do you see? You simply cannot do life wrong. It's all, every bit of it, an opportunity to say thank you. And, each time you do, your life gets bigger, it expands with more of what you want. Miracles abound!

And, YES, you will have days when you don't feel like saying thank you. And that's when you get to say **thank you for the fact that I do not want to say thank you right now**. AND, that's why it's a practice. You do it anyway. You get up in the morning and say thank you for this day, thank you for the miracles that will unfold today. And there will be days when you will say, FUCK GRATITUDE. Hell yes, YOU WILL. And it is OKAY. It's more than OKAY. It's part of gratitude. Thank you. Thank you for all of it. You know why? Because gratitude is FOR you. Gratitude helps you align with your true self, the essence of who you are. And, when you are aligned with your essence—YOUR JOY—you FEEL GOOD! Can I get an AMEN? Yes!

You get to feel good in this thing called life. YES. YOU. DO. You can start by saying thank you for everything. That's the practice. Thank you in the morning. Thank you in the afternoon. Thank you in the evening. Thank you all damn day! Thank you. Thank you for me. Thank you for you. Thank you for my feelings, all of them. Thank you for my thoughts, the ones that feel good and the ones that don't, choosing to believe they all SERVE me. Thank you for my body. Thank you for my sight. Thank you for my hearing. Thank you for my tasting. Thank you.

Saying thank you is not a Band-Aid to cover up or NOT feel unpleasant feelings. Feel the shitty stuff. FEEL IT. And when you're ready, simply say thank you. It raises your vibration and you FEEL BETTER. Your feeling better will make those around you feel better AND will draw more of what you want to you. I told ya—miracle maker. Let's practice!

PRACTICING GRATITUDE

What You'll Need:

- ☑ Quiet space @ the end of the day
- ☑ 15 minutes
- ☑ 3x5 index cards
- ☑ Journal/paper and pen
- ☑ Be-YOU-tiful YOU

Day 1 Gratitude

In order to be grateful, it's important to begin to notice. So today's practice is about noticing. Today you get to notice your feelings—when you are annoyed, frustrated, angry, happy, peaceful, free—that's it. Just notice your feelings. It may be helpful to write the statement, *Today's practice is to notice my feelings,* on a 3x5 index card to carry with you throughout the day to remind you of your practice. At the end of your day, take 10 minutes to reflect. Did you remember to notice your feelings? When you did, what feelings were they? Did any of them surprise you? Do you remember having any thoughts about having the feelings? Write down in your journal any thoughts or feelings that you receive in response to these questions.

Day 2 Gratitude

We all get in ruts and just mindlessly go through the motions. Not today. Today is about raising your awareness of the positive things that you may tend to overlook. Today, when you notice what is "right" or "good" in your world, say to yourself or out loud, **Thank you**. It may be helpful to write the statement, *Notice what's good in my life today and say thank you,* on a 3x5 index card to carry with you throughout the day. At the end of your day, take 10 minutes to reflect on your experience. What did you notice today that was good? Was it difficult for you to take notice? Was it more than you expected? Anything surprising? What were the associated feelings to your noticing what was good in your life? Write down in your journal any thoughts or feelings that you receive in response to these questions.

Day 3 Gratitude

Before you even get out of a bed, you have things to be grateful for that you are probably not aware of and may never have thought about before. So, tonight, put your journal or notepad by your bed. Upon waking, instead of reaching for your cell phone or looking at a clock, grab your pen and journal and write down three things for which you are grateful or you appreciate in THAT moment. Then, at the end of your day, review what you wrote in your journal that morning, and add your insights about the day. Did being grateful immediately upon waking change your outlook the rest of the day? Did you have trouble thinking of things to be grateful for? How did you feel today? Jot down any thoughts about the experience.

Day 4 Gratitude

Reflecting on and appreciating our days, our hours, our moments is a practice that can help you become more conscious of just how precious is this life we have been given. Continue with the Day 3 practice of writing three things down immediately upon waking and add three things at the end of this day that you are grateful for or appreciate in your life. Journal about your experience today. What were you grateful for today? Good things and not so good?

Are you starting to notice more things to be grateful for? Are you beginning to see how being grateful impacts you? How is it impacting you? How do you feel right now? Write down any thoughts or feelings you receive in response to these questions.

Day 5 Gratitude

Today is about intentionally appreciating the negative things as being a part of the goodness of our lives. Today, notice when things don't go your way or as you had planned, and notice the feelings you have in these moments. When you notice these times, say to yourself, **Thank you for this person | experience | feeling | thought. I know that this is happening FOR me. My life expands from here.** Repeat throughout the day, **MY LIFE EXPANDS FROM HERE. THANK YOU.** It may be helpful to write down the statement, *My life expands from here, thank you,* on a 3x5 index card to carry with you throughout the day to remind you of your practice. At the end of your day, write about your experience. How did you handle the negative moments? How did it feel to say thank you for them? Were you able to say thank you for them? How do you feel right now? Write down in your journal any thoughts or feelings you receive in response to these questions.

Day 6 Gratitude

Today you are going to verbalize your gratitude to someone who is important in your life. Today, choose one person. Call that person. Try not to leave a message–try to speak to them. Share with this person something you appreciate about them or what they have meant to you in your life. At the end of your day, take 10 minutes to reflect upon your experience. Was it difficult to reach out to this person? How did the person respond? How did you feel about your interaction with this person? Did you remember to say thank you for the experience no matter what? Write down any thoughts or feelings you receive in response to these questions.

Day 7 Gratitude

Wake up saying **Thank you**. Say it all damn day. About everything and to everyone. **Thank you**. Dog pooped in the house? **Thank you**. Baby vomit on you? **Thank you**. Slow traffic? **Thank you**. It may be helpful to write down the statement, *Say thank you no matter what all day long,* on a 3x5 index card to carry with you throughout your day to remind you of your practice. At the end of your day, reflect on your day. What was it like to say thank you all day long? Was it fun? Was it tiring? Did you get a kick out of it? Did you share what you were doing with others? How did that go? Write down in your journal any thoughts or feelings you receive in response to these questions. Thank you!

Element: **COMPASSION**

Core Belief: **Self-Love is the highest &
             greatest form of service.**

Practice: **Love Yourself Up!**

*You yourself, as much as anybody in the entire universe,
deserve your love and affection.*

~Buddha

•———————•

What is compassion? Compassion is a love for all. And it feels SO good. How do you get a love for all? Compassion grows through a love of self. The practice for Compassion is LOVE YOURSELF UP! Loving and appreciating yourself grows from the inside. What's that you say? You were not taught to love yourself? Perhaps you received the message at some point along the way–or all along the way–that it is most loving to be self-LESS.

Well, here's the deal: When there is no SELF in you, then you are what? You are EMPTY. Learning to truly LOVE yourself is you embracing your WHOLENESS. Not your emptiness. It is really brave to decide to love yourself. Why is this? Well, on your way to loving your-self–to your wholeness–you most likely will experience

THE GAP. Or, I've had clients refer to it as the hole. The gap or the hole lives inside you, lives inside me, lives inside us all. The gap is painful. It's painful because the gap is hungry and insatiable. FILL ME, it screams! The gap usually shows up as need...the need to feel safe, valued, appreciated, or loved. Relying on others solely to fill your gap will continue to cause suffering. Why? Because whenever you rely on a source outside of yourself to fill you up, you are always going to be unsatisfied. Others cannot fill your gap. And it is not their job.

The salve for the ache is Self-Love–learning to tap into the love that is inherent in YOU. To venture this way is not necessarily comfy. Allowing the love that is YOU to embrace YOU is an extremely vulnerable act. To love the self? What if this love is not enough? What if I–as in Me, Myself, and I–can't even love ME? Yes, it is vulnerable. It is raw. AND, so very worth it. Loving yourself will get you to compassion for YOU, which will naturally get you to Compassion for ALL. And Compassion FEELS SO GOOD!!! When you begin to truly love yourself from the inside out, the gap begins to close and you are free. You will notice a caring, a kindness, a gentleness...toward YOURSELF. And this care, kindness, and gentleness will then extend to others, all others. And it feels so freaking GOOD!!

How do you begin to love yourself? At the salon where I get my hair cut, there's a sign that says, DO SOME-THING EVERY DAY THAT MAKES YOU HAPPY.

Only one thing a day?!? Loving yourself is being kind and caring with yourself in each MOMENT. Not once a day. Yes! When you are living in a state of compassion for yourself, all of your choices align with LOVE. In order to be the best you can be for others, you've got to first be the best you can be for YOU. With a solid foundation of Me-ness, you can bring your fully empowered and WHOLE self to life and to all of your relationships. The practice of self-love helps you do this. This week is about being in the question of: How can I best nourish | care for | love myself today? The love you seek is already inside of you...so this practice is simply about connecting with the love that YOU ALREADY ARE. Eventually you will connect to the deep and enduring love that IS YOU. At that point, the love that is you will be brimming over and you will not be able to contain it and people will wonder what the heck you are doing differently. True Self-Love = True Love for All.

Our family once had a dog named Kirby. Kirby was not with us long but he sure did teach us a lot. What I noticed about Kirby is that he knew how to get his needs met and he did it with gusto. Kirby ate when he was hungry (many times using his own devices to get food!), he lapped up water when he was thirsty, he would sit down and pant when he needed a rest, he would break out of our yard when he needed adventure, and he would sleep hard when he was tired. He also gave kisses when he needed some love. Kirby did not wait to get what he needed. Yes, we had to put his food and water out, but he took it upon himself for the most part to get his needs met...to LOVE HIMSELF.

Wow. Just think if we could all do that...take care of ourselves. Nurture ourselves. Love ourselves. What do you need today? Allow your needs to be met. Perhaps it's having a conversation, holding someone's hand, taking a bike ride, or asking for help. Or, maybe taking five minutes to breathe. Slowly. In and out. Ask: How can I nurture myself this week, this day, this moment? Do it! The idea of self-care and nurture may be challenging for you. If this is so and you don't know where or how to start, simply go toward that which delights you, brings you pleasure, and makes you feel alive. If you don't know or are unsure how to go about this, it's okay! All you need to do is ASK. Yes. Just say aloud: Help me go toward that which I love, that which delights me, and that which makes my heart and soul sing! Let's practice!

PRACTICING COMPASSION

What You'll Need:

- ☑ Quiet space @ the end of the day
- ☑ 15 minutes
- ☑ 3x5 index cards
- ☑ Journal/paper and pen
- ☑ Be-YOU-tiful YOU

Day 1 Compassion

Today is simply about noticing your preferences. What do you like? Maybe you don't know what you truly like. It's okay! Remember the movie *Runaway Bride*? Julia Roberts did not know her preferences, including how she liked her eggs, because she always assumed the preferences of her significant other. So there is a scene where she is making all kinds of eggs—scrambled, poached, sunny-side up, an omelet—how do you like your eggs? What do you prefer? When faced with choices today—whether it's what to eat, or whether you like the blinds open or closed, or what music is playing on the radio—just notice what you are drawn to and what pleases you. Make today about just noticing instead of walking through your day unaware of what you want. Not only is it okay to have likes and dislikes—favorite things that bring us joy—but preferences are a key component of self-care. In fact, they help make us who we are! As we begin to know and choose our preferences, we begin to fall in love with ourselves. We start to see that these are the unique leanings that shape our individual personalities. It might be helpful to write the statement, *Today is about noticing my preferences,* on a 3x5 index card to carry with you throughout the day. At the end of your day, take 10 minutes to reflect. Did it feel strange to notice your own preferences? Was it difficult to know what you like or dislike? Did it feel uncomfortable or silly? Or maybe you found you have some quirky tastes? Whatever your experience was, describe it in your journal.

Day 2 Compassion

First thing after you get out of bed this morning, go to the mirror. Ask yourself aloud, **How can I nourish myself today?** Notice what comes up for you as you ask this question. No matter what comes up, say thank you. It might be helpful to write the question, *How can I nourish myself today,* on a 3x5 index card to carry with you throughout your day to remind yourself. Notice how your day unfolds from here. At the end of your day, take 10 minutes to reflect. Did you receive an answer or answers? Did you follow the guidance you received? Did anything surprise you? Write down any thoughts or feelings you receive in response to these questions in your journal.

Day 3 Compassion

Notice the tapes–those continuous thoughts–that are playing in your head. We all have them. They form the background of our lives without us even realizing their impact on our emotional health. Comments directed at us from our childhood, lies we've told ourselves, ideas we've held all our lives. It might be helpful to take your journal with you as you go about your day so that you can write down what you notice as it happens. How do your "tapes" feel to you? Do they uplift you or deflate you? Are they negative and condemning? Or maybe you're having an imaginary argument with someone you know–a conversation you'll never actually have in real life. Notice all of these background thoughts today, and then at the end of your day, read what you wrote about during the day and add anything else that comes to you. What did your daily tapes consist of? Where did your mind involuntarily go when it was "at rest"? At the end of your day, review what you wrote down and see if you can gain any insights into your thought patterns.

Day 4 Compassion

Today's practice is about letting negative thoughts pass through you so that you do not keep them inside unlooked at, unexperienced, and suppressed. It's about having compassion and gentleness in the way you process your own thoughts so that they cannot have power over you. When you notice a thought that deflates you or is stressful, speak to that thought. Say something like: **I hear you and thank you for your service in my life. I'm ready to move on to other thoughts now that inspire and uplift me. You are free to rest now.** It might be helpful to write that statement on a 3x5 index card and carry it with you today as a reference point. At the end of your day, take 10 minutes to reflect on your experience. How did it feel to speak to your negative thoughts? Silly? Empowering? Freeing? Write down all thoughts and feelings that come to you as a result of these questions.

Day 5 Compassion

Today is about beginning to replace the old tapes with a new soundtrack. Today is the day to actively choose kind words to speak to you. Choose gentle, loving words that uplift and inspire you, body, heart, and soul. Say to yourself numerous times and for no reason: **You can do it. You are so brave. You are enough. I love you.** Begin by saying these things to yourself in the mirror. You may want to write down these statements on a 3x5 card to carry with you throughout the day as you learn to speak lovingly to YOU. Add any other excellent thoughts that come into your awareness. At the end of your day, take 10 minutes to reflect. How did it feel to repeat these loving words to yourself? Natural? Unnatural? That's okay if it did—just keep doing it. It gets easier the more you do it and you're going to LOVE YOURSELF like crazy before long.

Day 6 Compassion

Our practice today is about awakening hope and possibility. Get up, go to the mirror, and ask yourself aloud, **What would I do today if I wasn't afraid?** Give yourself quiet time, 5 to 10 minutes, to allow the answer to surface. Allow all of the feelings and thoughts and visions that rise up with this question and write them down in your journal. It might also be helpful to write the question down on your handy index card or somewhere you will see it to remind yourself throughout the day to be mindful of what you would do if you weren't afraid. Then go about your day, revisiting the question throughout the day. At the end of your day, take 10 minutes to reflect and write down any additional answers that surfaced for you. Look at what you wrote down. Did anything surface that you did not expect? Did you have difficulty thinking of things? Or was it easy? How did this exercise feel to you? Journal your thoughts, feelings, and insights.

Day 7 Compassion

Make sure your schedule allows flexibility on the day you do this practice. Today is about loving yourself by going toward that which brings you pleasure and delights you– all day long! Let go of what you "should" do and who you "should" be and just be YOU. Literally lose the agenda. Let Joy–your inner compass–steer you today. Love yourself up by choosing what makes you giddy and delighted! Do you always drive the most direct way to where you are going? Perhaps today you choose the scenic route simply because it makes you smile. Do you normally exercise in the evening? Perhaps today you do it in the morning, simply because that's what feels good to you. Be easy. Be gentle. Loving yourself takes time. At the end of your day, take 10 minutes to reflect. How did it feel to simply follow your heart today? Was it uncomfortable to allow yourself so much freedom? Write down in your journal any thoughts and feelings about your experience today.

Element: **ABUNDANCE**

Core Belief: **I am enough; I matter**

Practice: **Receive the Gift of YOU**

Act as if what you do makes a difference. It does.

~William James

• ———— •

You are the gift! You being you is a gift! Do you know this?! Abundance is about knowing you are the gift, owning this, and ROCKING your gift! What is abundance? Abundance is enough. In fact, abundance is more than enough, right? So, when applied to you, it is YOU knowing you are more than ENOUGH. Abundance is value...knowing your value, not intellectually in your MIND, but in your BONES. Do you know your value? Do you own it? Do you share it?

Knowing, owning, and sharing your value–the gift of YOU–is abundance. You matter! Do you know this? Do you act as if you matter? Do you ever dismiss or deny yourself, your value, and what you bring to the world? It's okay if you've done this or do this. Remember, love yourself by giving yourself a break. You don't have to beat yourself up about this. Shoot, I've done it and sometimes still do.

About a year after I got my creativity studio, a man I did not know visited me. He was looking for someone to create a custom piece to commemorate his wedding anniversary. It was to be a gift for his wife. I found myself beginning to direct him to the place across the street. I wasn't computing that he could possibly be looking for me. He had to stop me mid-sentence and say, "No, this is the place. I came here a week ago and you weren't here, but I looked in the windows. This is it. You are it."

Wow. Okay. I went on to complete the project for him and it was such an amazingly cool experience. What is most amazingly cool is that when I look back on it, I see that I almost sent my Abundance—my value—across the street. Here was someone coming to me, who saw my value, but I did not see what he saw. That day taught me about OWNING MY ABUNDANCE, my value. When I don't own my value, it does not feel good to me. It does not feel good because when you do this, you are shushing a vital part of yourself. You are shushing your MAGIC! The miracle of You!

The practice for Abundance is to RECEIVE THE GIFT OF YOU. What does this mean? When you are living in abundance, you know, own, and share WHO YOU ARE with the world. Your *who-you-areness* is your VALUE. You may be thinking, *But isn't GIVING the most important thing?* Yes! Giving is AWESOME!! And, the more you are able to RECEIVE the GIFT OF YOU, the more you are able to share who you are with others! Giving and receiving are part of the SAME circle...the ABUNDANCE circle. Until we truly RECEIVE the gift of who we are, we can't GIVE all of who we are.

.————.

Until we truly RECEIVE the gift of who we are,
we can't GIVE all of who we are

.————.

As you learn to fully receive the gift of YOU, you are simultaneously learning to fully GIVE the gift of YOU. And, as they say in Vegas, winner, winner, chicken dinner! When I feel insignificant, like I don't matter, I want to duck my head and go hide in a closet. I know better. I know that I matter. I know that I make a difference by being in the world. I know better. And, it doesn't change the feeling of insignificance when it comes up in me. So, first I allow the feeling to emerge...to give it the space to BE because IT IS. When you deny your feelings a space to BE, you are denying a part of you. Allowing your feelings is one way that you RECEIVE the gift of YOU. Your feelings are a part of you, and therefore, are valuable.

As an example, about a year ago I experienced the full force of an emotion I could not name. It started as a tiny rumble and ended up feeling like a pressure on my chest. The pressure felt like FEAR and it was palpable. It was physical. I was so afraid. And, yet, I knew there was something in me that wanted to come out and needed to be expressed. Something in me was clamoring to be FELT.

Feel me! it shouted. I surrendered. I allowed myself to pass through the Fear and feel it. It wasn't as bad as I thought. I have found that settling in and making my home with fear is always far worse than the thing I was imagining. With some help, I was able to identify what I was feeling as INSIGNIFICANT.

As a numerologist, I often add up the letters in a word to see what number I will get. When I added up "Insignificant," I got 71, which in numerology is an 8. An 8! And wouldn't you know that the number 8 represents ABUNDANCE and POWER? I love this so much. In order to truly OWN YOUR VALUE, you need to be able to FEEL your insignificance. In feeling your insignificance you unlock your POWER. How? Whenever you feel, you are allowing yourself to connect to your heart. The heart heals…When something such as insignificance connects with the healing power of the heart, transformation happens. Allow yourself to connect to the awareness that who you are matters, yes it does! Your value is who you are and the gift you are to the world. When you fully RECEIVE the gift of who you are, you are able to fully share YOU, confidently, and with no apologies. And everyone wins! Let's practice!

PRACTICING ABUNDANCE

What You'll Need:

- ☑ Quiet space @ the end of the day
- ☑ 15 minutes
- ☑ 3x5 index cards
- ☑ Journal/paper and pen
- ☑ Be-YOU-tiful YOU

Day 1 Abundance

Upon waking this morning, get up and go to the mirror and say, **Today, I start where I am**. What does this mean? It means you give yourself a break—it's not about spending time in the past, beating yourself up about your perceived challenges and failures. None of that matters anymore. The gift of allowing yourself to start where you are is about a clean slate. Right here. Right now. You are at square one. Simply take the first step. Allow yourself to release all thought of "what's next?" Take the first step. Allow yourself to know that you have everything within you that you need. You are enough. Start where you are. Throughout the day, in each moment, repeat: **I START WHERE I AM**. It may be helpful to write this statement on a 3x5 index card or somewhere that you can see it throughout your day to remind you to start where you are. At the end of the day, find a quiet space and reflect on your experience. How did repeating this phrase affect you today? What does it mean to you to start where you are?

Were you able to find a fresh start in your thoughts? Write down in your journal any thoughts or feelings that come up for you as a result of these questions.

Day 2 Abundance

Today, when you get up, look in the mirror and say: **I am significant. I matter.** Allow the feelings that these statements bring up in you to surface. Honor the feelings by feeling them, and try not to judge them. Notice if you can look at yourself when you say these words or not. There is not good or bad. Just awareness. Notice. Allow all of the thoughts and feelings to come up. Whatever they are. Say it again. **I AM SIGNIFICANT. I MATTER.** Make this your mantra for the day. It might be helpful to write this affirmation down on a 3x5 index card or somewhere you will see it throughout the day. When you believe in your bones that you are significant and that you matter, you can authentically be in relationship with others in that same space...everyone is significant and matters. Say it throughout the day, **I AM SIGNIFICANT. I MATTER.** At the end of the day, find a quiet space and reflect. How did it feel to say this to yourself? Awkward? Difficult? Good? Did it get easier as the day went on? Jot down any thoughts or feelings about how this experience of saying, I am significant, I matter, was for you.

Day 3 Abundance

Today, when you get up, say to yourself, in the mirror: **My presence has a meaningful impact on those around me.** Imagine an inner glow emanating from within you as you go about your day today, repeating the words, **MY PRESENCE HAS A MEANINGFUL IMPACT ON THOSE AROUND ME,** and beginning to believe it in your heart. Write down this statement on an index card or somewhere you will see it throughout the day. At the end of the day, find a quiet space and reflect. Were you able to visualize your inner glow issuing forth to your surroundings and to others? How did you experience yourself today as you repeated it? Did you begin to believe it? Do you believe it? Write down any thoughts and feelings that come up for you in response to these questions.

Day 4 Abundance

Today, look in the mirror and ask yourself, **How can I share who I am with others?** As your day unfolds, ask yourself along the way, **HOW CAN I SHARE MYSELF RIGHT NOW?** Write this question down on your index card if you think it would be helpful to you in remembering it throughout the day. At the end of the day, find a quiet space and reflect. Did any ideas come up for you as to how to share yourself? It's okay if they did not. How was it to ask yourself this question? How did it feel? Perhaps just by asking yourself the question, you were able to be more authentically you in each moment with the people in your life? Did you find this to be true? This can come in all forms…it can be a word of encouragement from you to another. It can look like helping someone in some way. Or it can simply be asking someone how they are doing, or sharing a smile. Write down in your journal any thoughts or feelings that these questions bring up for you.

Day 5 Abundance

Today, when you get up, say to yourself in the mirror: **I don't need to prove anything. My being in the world is valuable. Me, just being me, is valuable**. Say this several more times, each time with more conviction and truth. Shout it, if it feels good. Keep this mantra with you throughout the day: **ME, JUST BEING ME, IS VALUABLE.** Write this statement down on an index card or somewhere you will see it throughout the day. At the end of the day, find a quiet space and reflect. What was it like to carry this thought in your heart and mind today? How did this thought affect how you went about your day? Did you feel the truth of this thought resonate in your bones? Write down in your journal any thoughts and feelings you have in response to these questions.

Day 6 Abundance

We can get into a blind rut, going through our days without realizing we have choices in how we think and how we approach life. Today, when you get up, ask yourself in the mirror, **Believing I am enough, what will I do, or do differently, today?** Carry this question with you throughout the day. Write it on an index card or somewhere you will see it to remind yourself to be in this question today. See what unfolds. At the end of your day, find a quiet space and reflect. Any insights? Did it change your perspective? Did it impact your typical routine? How did you experience yourself today? Confident? Powerful? Sure of yourself? Or not so much? Write down any thoughts or feelings that come up for you in response to these questions.

Day 7 Abundance

Feeling insignificant and therefore powerless is a deception. The truth is, we each have a power lying within us to create the thoughts we want and the life we want. Today, when you get up, say to yourself in the mirror: **I own my power. I own my worth. I own my value. In every word. In every action. In every thought. In every feeling. I own my power. I own my worth.** In order to remember this thought throughout the day, you can shorten it to, **TODAY I OWN MY POWER**, and you can write it down somewhere you will see it to remind you throughout the day. At the end of the day, find a quiet space and reflect. Your abundance–WHO YOU ARE–is your power. Did you experience yourself owning your power–who you are–today? This could look like voicing your opinion about something, especially when it's hard. It could be allowing yourself to feel an unpleasant feeling or a really jubilant feeling. It's different for everyone because each one of us is uniquely who we are. Write down any thoughts or feelings you get in response to these questions.

Element: **PEACE**

Core Belief: **I can cultivate internal peace**

Practice: **Breathe**

Peace is flowing like a river, flowing out of you and me.
Flowing out into the desert, setting all the captives free.

~Michael O'Brien

—————

There is an internal flow within you: the river of peace. And when you intentionally step into the flow, there is a calmness there. Outside the flow there can be agitation and anxiety. You know the feeling—you are trying to get the kids out the door and onto the bus in time. Or, you've got a work deadline that you are not sure you are going to make. Or, you have ten people coming over for a dinner party and you want everything to be *just so*. Feel the chaos and anxiety, of course, if it rises up in you. And then, KNOW that you have the power to FREE yourself in each moment.

In any moment, you have the power to step out of the chaos and connect to the river of peace that flows within you. How? The practice is to BREATHE. Yes. Breathe. In and out. Just breathe. When you connect to your breath, you are connecting to life. Life that is bigger than you, bigger than your understanding. Breath is Life. Breath is ALIVE!! When you breathe for even five minutes in the morning–*taking in what you need* with the in-breath and *letting out that which is ready to be released* with the out-breath–it is enough. Then, during the day, if and when you feel yourself start to spiral–spiraling feels like panic, anxiety, chaos, fear–feel it. And then, pause. Remember the power you have to choose. Take a deep breath. Breathe. In and out. Breathe.

Why does it work? When you breathe you are stilling the mind–it is difficult to concentrate on the breath AND think at the same time. Focusing on the breath results in intentional mind-quieting. When you quiet the mind, you are able to transcend to another dimension and connect with your higher self, a place where all of those mental constructs–the conditioning of your life–the shoulds, the shouldn'ts, and who you think you have to be–do not exist. The breath enables us to see that if we miss the bus, we can take the kids to school. If we don't make the deadline, we are not going to die and the world will not come to a halt. And, the dinner party will be fine. There is a reason people count to ten before responding. The ten seconds is not so much about the counting but the breathing. The breath calms you by connecting to the river of peace that runs through you. By taking a few minutes a day to intentionally breathe in and out, you are giving yourself an opportunity to bypass the paradigms that perhaps constrain and constrict you, and you can find peace.

A personal example of mine is that I used to carry a lot of anger. When my anger was triggered, my automatic response was to yell. I did this for many years. It had become my habit. I was not connected to my river of peace. Eventually, I became conscious that yelling did not feel good—it did not feel good within me to yell. I began to slowly replace this habit with a new response, which was to breathe. Know that anytime you feel agitated—perhaps it's watching the news or when you've had too much Facebook or superficial conversations—you have a choice. You can stay in this state of agitation, or you can choose Peace by connecting with your breath. Let's practice.

PRACTICING PEACE

What You'll Need:

- ☑ Quiet space @ the beginning of the day
- ☑ Quiet space @ the end of the day
- ☑ 3x5 index cards
- ☑ Journal/paper and pen
- ☑ Be-YOU-tiful YOU

Day 1 Peace

Get up before anyone in your house. Find a quiet, comfortable spot. Set a timer for 5 minutes. Eyes open or closed, whichever is most comfortable. Begin breathing.

With each in-breath, imagine taking in what you need. With each out-breath, imagine that you are freeing what is ready to be released—anything negative, anything unpleasant, anything causing anxiety. With each breath, know that you are connecting to your river of peace. It is possible to take this into your day. Write out on an index card, *I take peace into my day,* and carry it with you where you can see it or access it at any time. Maybe the dashboard of your car, or taped to your computer. At the end of the day, take 10 minutes to reflect. How did doing this exercise in the morning impact your day? Were you able to take peace into your day? How did the exercise feel to you? How do you feel now? Use your journal to write down any thoughts or feelings that come up for you in response to these questions.

Day 2 Peace

Continue the practice for Day 1. Additionally, say the following into the mirror when you get up and throughout your day: **I am peace. I connect to my peace through the breath.** Write down this affirmation on an index card or somewhere you can access it easily throughout the day. *I am peace. I connect to my peace through the breath.* See how your day unfolds. At the end of your day, take 10 minutes to reflect. Were you able to feel the peace within you during your day? Perhaps you were even more agitated? If this was the case for you, it is okay and perfectly normal. Almost always, when you want to experience a new way of being, like peace, you will experience more of the opposite of it, like anxiety and agitation, as you work your way to that new way of being. How did you feel during your day? How do you feel now? Is it helpful to you to tap into your peace river throughout the day? Use your journal to write down all thoughts and feelings you receive in response to these questions.

Day 3 Peace

Continue the practice for Day 1. Additionally, find 5 minutes *during your day*. Set a timer. Begin to breathe. Imagine taking in what you need with every in-breath and letting go of that which you no longer need with the out-breath. No judgments; you can't do this wrong. Imagine the river of peace getting stronger in you with every breath you take. Imagine taking this peace into your day. At the end of the day, take 10 minutes to reflect. Write any thoughts and feelings that come to you about your day. Are you becoming more aware of the peace that resides within you?

Day 4 Peace

Continue the practice for Days 1 and 3. Additionally, say the following into the mirror when you get up: **I am peace. Even in the midst of chaos, I can access my peace at any time by pausing and breathing.** Say it to yourself several times more and as you do consciously speak to yourself as you would a dear friend, with love and kindness. Carry these thoughts with you throughout the day. Write them on your index card so that you will be reminded of your practice. At the end of your day, reflect on your experience. How did you feel today? What thoughts came to you that were new or different? How did peace show up for you? Reflecting on how you feel and becoming conscious of your thoughts, noticing if those thoughts and feelings feel good or if they feel bad, are an important piece of connecting to Joy–becoming more YOU. Write in your journal any insights or connections you made today.

Day 5 Peace

Continue the practice for Days 1 and 3. Additionally, find 5 minutes *at the end of your day*. Find a quiet space where you will not be disturbed. Set a timer. Begin to breathe. Imagine taking in what you need with every in-breath and letting go of that which you no longer need with the out-breath. See the river of peace in your mind's eye. However you can picture it, see yourself flowing along with the current of peace. When your 5 minutes is complete, write about any insights. How is taking a few minutes to breathe in the morning, the middle of the day, and at the end of the day impacting you? Are you noticing any changes in the way you feel, the way you interact with others, or your relationship with yourself?

Day 6 Peace

Continue the practice for Days 1, 3, and 5. Additionally, say the following into the mirror when you get up: **I am peace. My breath is my connection to peace. As I breathe today, I am peace.** Say it several more times and as you do, feel yourself connecting to the current of peace within you. Take this statement into your day by writing it on your index card and carrying it with you. *I am peace. My breath is my connection to peace. As I breathe today, I am peace.* At the end of the day, reflect on your experience. How did you feel today? Did you experience anxiety or frustration? If you did, did you acknowledge these feelings—allow them? Maybe you felt less of this and more calmness today? Joy is not about getting to any certain place or about not having negative feelings. It is about having all of the feelings you have and not holding onto them. Have them and let them go. Write down any thoughts and feelings you had today and right now.

Day 7 Peace

Continue the practice for Days 1, 3, and 5 and add 5 minutes so that you are breathing consciously three times today, for 10 minutes each time. As you lay your head on your pillow tonight, say to yourself, **I sleep in peace and wake in joy.** You may want to write this statement on an index card and put it on your pillow this morning so that you will remember tonight. You ARE peace. The breath is the doorway to your peace. By becoming conscious of your breath and breathing, you will feel more peace—you will become the peace that you ARE. Write now in your journal about any insights you had today or over the past seven days.

Element: **FREEDOM**

Core Belief: **Freedom lies in my ability to let go of what I thought it would be**

Practice: **Let go**

> *Why do you stay in prison when*
> *the door is so wide open?*
>
> ~Rumi

•———————•

Freedom IS. You are free. You just are. When you don't feel free it is because you are holding on to your idea or vision of a person, relationship, or situation that is just that...an IDEA. The ACTUAL person, relationship, or situation has changed or moved beyond your IDEA. And you are still back there, feeling not free because you are holding on to what WAS. You are creating your own misery, your own prison, by holding on.

When you can let go of what WAS, you open up a space to greet what IS. You can experience freedom when you let go of how you thought your life was going to be and embrace how and what it truly is. When you can take this concept and apply it from moment to moment, you are creating a practice of letting go.

As a simple example, let's say you have agreed with the babysitter that she is to come at 6:30 p.m. But she doesn't come at 6:30 p.m. She comes at 7 p.m. Resisting what is actually happening, the fact that she is 30 minutes late, will create feelings of strife within you. Resisting looks like judging, blaming, shaming—which creates feelings of frustration, anger, or sadness. When these feelings occur, and they will, witness them—and let them go. This will launch you into a space of possibility and then FREEDOM. Because you are no longer holding onto your picture of what WAS. This does not mean you do not have a conversation with the babysitter. No. I am not suggesting you let people walk all over you. That is not what I'm talking about here. This is about your FREEDOM. As always, feel what you are feeling. Notice all of it...your thoughts and your feelings. And then let go.

———

Freedom is about welcoming it all and then noticing what resonates with you, what lights you up, and then CHOOSING THAT!

———

How? Say, *I'm ready to let go. I am free.* Surrender what you are holding onto to allow what wants to be a place to BE. Freedom. We are the only ones who can imprison ourselves. WE do it through our thoughts. So, choose thoughts that feel good to you. That bring you lightness and joy. That fill you up. This is not denial. Freedom is about welcoming it all and then noticing what resonates with you, what lights you up, and then CHOOSING THAT! Let's practice!

PRACTICING FREEDOM

What You'll Need:

- ☑ Quiet space @ the end of the day
- ☑ 15 minutes
- ☑ 3x5 index card
- ☑ Journal/paper and pen
- ☑ Be-YOU-tiful YOU

Day 1 Freedom

Freedom feels, well, free. You are in charge of feeling free. You have the power to choose Freedom. In order to FEEL free, you must release yourself from any of the boxes that confine you and feel constricting. You can do this in each moment. Today, you get to practice releasing yourself to Joy. So, get up! Go to your bathroom mirror and say: **I release this day to Joy! Moment to moment, I let go of what WAS and receive what IS!** Say it several times in the mirror, each time with more feeling and power. As the day goes on, remind yourself: **MOMENT TO MOMENT, I LET GO OF WHAT WAS AND RECEIVE WHAT IS.** Write this affirmation on your index card and carry it with you throughout the day to remind yourself. *Moment to moment, I let go of what WAS and receive what IS!* At the end of your day, take 10 minutes to reflect. What did you experience today? What was it like for you to be in the moment and let go of what you thought something would be like to embrace what actually WAS happening in the moment? Were you able to do this? Was it difficult? Write down in your journal any thoughts or feelings that come in response to these questions.

Day 2 Freedom

The feeling of Freedom requires that we are open to the possibilities of each moment, letting go of what we thought someone or something was going to be and opening up to the gift of what IS. Today you get to practice further opening yourself to feeling free. So, get up! Go to your bathroom mirror and say to yourself: **I do not know the specifics of what this day holds. What I do know is that everything is about expansion. I expand into the infiniteness that I am. I am free.** Say this several times over, feeling more alive and free with each repetition. Write down the phrase: *I am free*, on your card and take it with you during the day to remind you of your practice. At the end of your day take 10 minutes to reflect. What was it like to release yourself to the infiniteness that you are? How did you feel today? Did you feel expansive? Did you feel free? Did you feel the opposite—stuck, restricted, or limited? It's okay. Whatever you felt. Everything fits and it's all valid. The important part is to notice. Write down in your journal any thoughts or feelings you have in response to these questions.

Day 3 Freedom

A key component to feeling free is letting go of the thoughts–the mental constructs–that no longer feel good to you. Today you get to practice noticing the mental constructs that keep you stuck. When you get up, say to yourself in the mirror, **Today, I lovingly notice the mental constructs that do not feel good to me. I know that in my noticing, they are beginning to dissolve. I am free.** Say this several more times with resolve and clarity. Write on one of your cards the phrase, *I am free,* and bring it with you to remind yourself throughout the day. At the end of your day, let yourself reflect on your experience. How did it go today? Were you able to notice any thoughts that did not feel good to you? What was this like? Write down in your journal any thoughts or feelings that come to you in response to these questions.

Day 4 Freedom

Today, you are again going to notice your thoughts. Especially the ones that seem to cause an unpleasant response in you, such as annoyance, frustration and anger. Once you notice them, the second part of today's practice is to let yourself feel the feelings. Stay with it. Feeling your feelings takes a lot of courage, mostly because those so-called negative feelings don't feel good. As you are feeling your feelings, see if you notice any urge to "disown" or "push out" your feelings onto others (instead of feeling them) in the form of blame, shame, judgment, or criticism. This is very important. There is the potential for a very large shift in your life toward feeling BETTER when you can take responsibility for your own feelings and not inflict them onto others. Today, write on your index card the phrase: *I let myself feel my negative feelings.* Take this card with you today to remind yourself of your practice. At the end of your day, give yourself some reflection time. What was today like for you? Were you able to stay with any negative feelings you had? What was that like? Did you notice that you ever wanted to disown or project your feelings outward toward someone else? What was that like? Write down in your journal any thoughts or feelings you receive in response to these questions.

Day 5 Freedom

Just because we have feelings doesn't mean that we actually FEEL them. Today's practice is to be really aware of how you are feeling. It might feel really strange to be this sensitive to your feelings. Stay with it. Notice all of your feelings, whatever they may be. Give yourself permission to pause throughout your day and breathe and observe—almost clinically as if noticing someone else. Before you start your day, say to yourself in the mirror and throughout your day: **I live in the now, I accept what comes.** It might be helpful to write this phrase on one of your index cards to carry with you throughout the day to remind you to live in the now, accepting all feelings as they come. At the end of your day, let yourself have some reflection time.

Are you finding yourself able to notice and feel your feelings? Have you had any insights or inspirations as you practice feeling your feelings? Were you able to feel your feelings, let them go, and move on about your day? Or, did you find yourself staying in your feelings for awhile? Write down in your journal any thoughts or feelings you get in response to these questions.

Day 6 Freedom

Today the practice is to let go, if only for a few minutes, of the thoughts that are causing you stress, and replace them with new thoughts, ones that FEEL better to you. For example, maybe you're in the coffee shop and the barista asks you your name to write on your coffee cup. You give them your name and you even spell it for them and you notice that they've spelled it wrong on the cup. Maybe your thought goes something like this, "That damn barista spelled my name wrong on my coffee cup. I hate it when that happens." Whatever your situation is and whatever your thought is, notice it. How do you feel? If the thought causes you stress, choose a new thought—one that feels better to you. In this instance, maybe it's something like: "It's nice they try to personalize my experience." It is self-love to choose a better-feeling thought (see #4 - Compassion). At the end of your day today, let yourself have some reflection time. Were you able to isolate your bad-feeling thoughts and then choose better-feeling thoughts? What was that like for you? Write down in your journal any thoughts or feelings you get in response to these questions.

Day 7 Freedom

Today you get to practice letting go even more. In each moment, see if you can let go of what you think life is supposed to be like and just accept what comes. Before you begin your day, look at yourself in the mirror and say: **It is safe to let go. I am supported. I am now feeling free**. You may want to use one of your index cards to jot this phrase down and bring with you to repeat to yourself throughout the day. At the end of your day, give yourself some time to reflect. How did you experience yourself today? How did you experience your interactions with others today? What does it mean to you to be and feel free? Write down in your journal any thoughts and feelings you receive in response to these questions.

Element: **VULNERABILITY**

Core Belief: **I am Held**

Practice: **Trust**

> *Those who are willing to be vulnerable*
> *move among mysteries.*
>
> ~Theodore Roethke

•———————•

You know the phrase, "It's such a small world"? The funny thing about this phrase is that it is NOT a small world. It is a very, very large world—seven billion people large—and yet, seeming synchronicities, serendipities, and coincidences happen all the time. Do you know why? It is because you are held. We are all held. And Vulnerability is about doing a free fall into that held space.

Vulnerability, as are all of the Joy practices, is a choice. Vulnerability is a willingness to "go off the script." I was reminded of this not too long ago at a retreat. I was asked to lead a three-hour session on Kindness. About two days beforehand, I sat down to "work on" the outline. I wrote some things down. I felt good about it. As the retreat began to unfold, there was so much new information! There was so much newness that was revealing itself that my mind started going crazy...I wondered how I would crunch all of this yummy goodness together and integrate it into my session. Each moment, it seemed, my senses would take in new information that my mind thought it needed to do something with. I finally surrendered and told myself that there was no way I was going to be able to "script" the session and that what this required was trust. Trust that, in the moment, I would say what was needed and wanted to be said. To trust that I was held.

Trust is the practice for Vulnerability. Vulnerability doesn't say, "Don't plan." It does say that at some point we get to stop managing, controlling, and manipulating, and simply RECEIVE that which wants to be expressed through us. This can be during a facilitated session such as what I described, how we are in relationship with our children, our spouse, our friends—even creating a business. Vulnerability calls that we TRUST there is something GREATER than we are, than our KNOWING, and that this something GREATER wants to be expressed through us...we are simply the vehicle. And, Vulnerability calls us to GET OURSELVES OUT OF THE WAY so that whatever it is, whether it's a session on kindness, being a parent, or running a business, can EXPRESS ITSELF.

Many people's addiction to planning and order is to mitigate feeling out of control. And we try to plan our way to feeling safe. What Vulnerability wants you to know is that you are safe. You are held. No matter what. Vulnerability asks you to lean into the vast expanse that is your life, that is your relationship with your child or spouse, that is that business you are creating, and do a FREE FALL... trusting that YOU ARE HELD. Because if you weren't, you would not be in the position you are in. Vulnerability is not weakness. Vulnerability is openness. An openness to allowing LIFE TO EXPRESS through you the way IT wants to.

Why would anyone want to do this, you may be wondering? Because, it makes life more magical, mysterious, and miraculous. Vulnerability is a lynchpin of JOY. About 15 years ago, I was asked to give a talk at the church we belonged to at the time. I love the lesson in vulnerability it gave me. The talk I was asked to give was on stewardship. You know, the "money" talk. I couldn't see why they would want me to do this talk and I almost said no. But something within me said, "Yes." And that something was vulnerability. Somewhere inside of me I was Trusting that I would be HELD. That didn't mean I didn't write out my talk. I did. But it also meant that I had to get my own self—my ego—out of the way in order to bring forth what wanted to be expressed through me. That talk ended up being so much fun! My willingness to be vulnerable connected me to Joy.

Vulnerability is of the soul. And your soul has your back. It just does. Your soul is holding you. Always. In all ways. Vulnerability doesn't need to "figure anything out first." Vulnerability's got this. You can lean into Vulnerability. I promise. You are Held. Vulnerability defies logic.

All the data and information in the world will not help you trust. Your Soul has your back. Trust. Let's practice.

PRACTICING VULNERABILITY

What You'll Need:

- ☑ Quiet space @ the end of the day
- ☑ 15 minutes
- ☑ 3x5 index card
- ☑ Journal/paper and pen
- ☑ Be-YOU-tiful YOU

Day 1 Vulnerability

Trust may seem counterintuitive to the logical brain. Your logic may tell you that a certain situation is okay, when something else is telling you that it is not. Know that trust does not need to replace logic–see if you can view it as another tool to use alongside logic. So today, when you wake up, go to your bathroom mirror and, looking into your eyes, say, **I am open to trust.** Say to yourself throughout the day: **I AM OPEN TO TRUST.** Let this be your first step to learning trust–just being open to it. You may want to write this phrase, *I am open to Trust,* on your index card to carry with you throughout the day. At the end of your day, find a quiet spot and reflect. What was it like to invite Trust in? Write down in your journal any thoughts and feelings that come up in response to this question.

Day 2 Vulnerability

The willingness to be vulnerable, to Trust, is big, badass stuff. You are doing great. Today, when you wake up, go to your bathroom mirror, and, looking into your eyes, say, **Today I trust**. Say to yourself throughout the day: **TODAY I TRUST.** Let this statement become a part of your thoughts, even if you don't understand it yet. Write it out on your index card and carry it with you through-out the day. At the end of your day, find your quiet place and reflect. What was it like for you to claim, *Today I trust?* Were you able to lean in to trusting? If you were, what was that like? Write down in your journal any insights and feel-ings you get in response to these questions.

Day 3 Vulnerability

Today is about actively trusting. Try to identify some-thing that you've been wanting to do or felt drawn to do—perhaps take a new class or ask a new friend to lunch or coffee—but your logic has talked you out of it. About a year ago, I finally walked into a new exercise studio. I had been walking by this studio for about two years until one day I just did it. That decision was a game changer for me—that one seemingly small move has brought me so much Joy! I trusted my "knowing" that said, **GO IN!** What is it for you? Do it today. Just jump in. At the end of your day, go to your quiet spot and reflect. Were you able to think of something that you wanted to do? Were you able to do it today? How did it feel to just leap? Did you feel better or worse for having leapt? What did you learn? How do you feel now? Write down in your journal any insights and feelings you get in response to these questions.

Day 4 Vulnerability

There's a part of you that subconsciously guides you when you're open to it. Some may call this intuition. Today we are going to nurture this voice. When you wake up today, go to your bathroom mirror and, looking into your eyes, say, **I trust my inner knowing—that part of me that is not logical, but knows when something is right or wrong for me.** Say to yourself throughout the day: **I TRUST MY INNER KNOWING.** Write this phrase down on one of your index cards to carry with you throughout your day. At the end of your day, find your quiet spot and reflect. Did you have any experiences today where this inner knowing arose to lead you? Write down in your journal any insights or feelings you get from this question.

Day 5 Vulnerability

Today is about making a different decision about something in your life that you have kept doing even though that thing you are doing does not feel good to you. You may characterize it as a mindless habit. This can be a small thing. For example, recently I was drinking my coffee when I had the realization that it just did not taste good. Right there on the spot I dumped it out. I realized I was drinking it out of habit and it did not feel good to me. In this instance, I wasn't deciding to not drink coffee forever, it was just about that moment. When you are truly in the moment, the future effortlessly creates itself. Trust that you KNOW even if you can't logically or intellectually explain your knowing. If you are doing something and it does not feel good to you, let it go. Stop that behavior. Trust. Again, this can be a small thing or a big thing. Often it is the small things that are actually REALLY big. Something will most probably pop right into your awareness. If it doesn't, it is okay. Simply be aware throughout the day for something to reveal itself to you. At the end of your day, go to your quiet spot and reflect on your experience. Did anything come to mind where you realized you had been on autopilot? Find any behavior you just didn't need anymore? What actions or habits did you become aware of today—even the okay ones? Write down in your journal any thoughts or feelings you receive from these questions.

·———·

If you are doing something and it does not feel good to you, let it go.

·———·

Day 6 Vulnerability

Today is about expression. Sit quietly this morning and, clearing your mind, bring into your awareness some-one who you have been wanting or needing to share something with—for example, how you feel about them or what they mean to you—but you haven't because you have let your logic steer you in a different direction. Today is your day for sharing how you feel, speaking the words that want and need to be expressed to a specific person in your life. These are words from the heart and soul, words that are sometimes difficult to say, because we fear the sentiment may not be returned, or we fear another person's reaction. Is there a truth that you have not spoken that wants and needs to be expressed to someone? Is there an "I love you" that wants to be spoken? Is there an "I was wrong and I'm sorry I hurt you" that needs to be said? Is there a "Will you please forgive me?" Maybe it's you who needs to express a hurt—perhaps it's, "What you said to me really hurt me." Only you know. At the end of your day, find your quiet spot. Reflect on the following questions. What was it like to finally speak what wanted to be said? Was it hard for you to say the words? What was the person's reaction? How do you feel about this experience? Write down any thoughts and feelings you get in your journal.

Day 7 Vulnerability

Today is learning to gratefully receive what others say about you and to selectively choose that which serves you, and equally, not holding onto anything that would cause you inner shame or condemnation. When you wake up today, go to your bathroom mirror and, looking into your eyes, say, **Owning my power, I am able to hear other**

people's opinions about me and my life, integrate what resonates, and let go of the rest. Say to yourself throughout the day: **I RECEIVE WHAT RESONATES, I LET GO OF THE REST.** Write this phrase down on one of your index cards so that you remember throughout your day. At the end of your day, go to your quiet place. Were you able to discern that which resonated with your spirit? Were you able to let other things slide off you without causing you turmoil? Did you observe your feelings without judgment? Write down any thoughts or feelings you get in your journal.

Creating Your Own
Joy Practice

The key to Joy is allowing life to evolve the way it wants to... I did not set out to create a practice for Joy. I had an experience that had me ask myself, "How did I do that?" And from that question, the adventure of remembering what JOY is for me unfolded. And, for me, this includes:

Claiming what I want (Creativity)

Feeling all of my feelings (Aliveness)

Allowing all aspects of life to show up (Possibility)

Saying thank you no matter what (Gratitude)

Loving myself (Compassion)

Receiving the gift of me (Abundance)

Breathing (Peace)

Letting go (Freedom)

Trusting (Vulnerability)

I would love it if these practices work for you, too. But more than anything, I hope that The Joy Practice inspires you to ask yourself, "What is my Joy?" Most probably there are already "practices" you have that, when you apply them, bring you into your natural state of Joy. And, it is just about coming into the awareness of what these are for you and then using them as a launch pad for more JOY!

The Joy Practice is not meant to be a rigid set of rules that you or I need to stick to or else we're doomed. No. I have bad days. Days when I don't feel good and I want to give up. I do! And then, I remember. The words "thank you," no matter what, come trailing into my awareness. And I breathe. And I can slowly feel possibility rising up in me and with it a feeling of lightness and expansion. This is available for you, too. Know this.

You are CREATIVITY. You are ALIVENESS. You are POSSIBILITY. You are GRATITUDE. You are COMPASSION. You are ABUNDANCE. You are PEACE. You are FREEDOM. You are VULNERABILITY.

Know this.

You are a beautiful being of mystical, magical light. The world needs your light. Shine it. Shine it brightly. Shine on. See it as your service to the world. We do. And we thank you.

I love you to the moon and back.